Theodore Martin

The Book of Ballads

Theodore Martin

The Book of Ballads

ISBN/EAN: 9783744775595

Printed in Europe, USA, Canada, Australia, Japan

Cover: Foto ©Thomas Meinert / pixelio.de

More available books at **www.hansebooks.com**

THE
BOOK OF BALLADS

EDITED BY

BON GAULTIER

AND ILLUSTRATED BY

DOYLE, LEECH, AND CROWQUILL

FOURTEENTH EDITION

WILLIAM BLACKWOOD AND SONS
EDINBURGH AND LONDON
MDCCCLXXXIV

All Rights reserved

CONTENTS.

Spanish Ballads.

	PAGE
THE BROKEN PITCHER, ...	3
DON FERNANDO GOMERSALEZ: FROM THE SPANISH — OF ASTLEY'S, ...	7
THE COURTSHIP OF OUR CID, ...	24

American Ballads.

THE FIGHT WITH THE SNAPPING TURTLE; OR, THE AMERICAN ST GEORGE:—	
FYTTE FIRST, ...	35
FYTTE SECOND, ...	39
THE LAY OF MR COLT:—	
STREAK THE FIRST, ...	45
STREAK THE SECOND, ...	47
THE DEATH OF JABEZ DOLLAR, ...	53
THE ALABAMA DUEL, ...	59
THE AMERICAN'S APOSTROPHE TO "BOZ," .	66

Miscellaneous Ballads.

THE STUDENT OF JENA,	75
THE LAY OF THE LEVITE,	80
BURSCH GROGGENBURG,	82
NIGHT AND MORNING,	87
THE BITER BIT,	89
THE MEETING,	92
THE CONVICT AND THE AUSTRALIAN LADY,	94
THE DOLEFUL LAY OF THE HONOURABLE I. O. UWINS,	98
THE KNYGHTE AND THE TAYLZEOUR'S DAUGHTER,	105
THE MIDNIGHT VISIT,	112
THE LAY OF THE LOVELORN,	118
MY WIFE'S COUSIN,	130
THE QUEEN IN FRANCE: An ancient Scottish Ballad:—	
Part I.,	135
Part II.,	143
THE MASSACRE OF THE MACPHERSON: From the Gaelic,	150
THE YOUNG STOCKBROKER'S BRIDE,	155
THE LAUREATES' TOURNEY:—	
Fytte the First,	159
Fytte the Second,	165
THE ROYAL BANQUET,	169
THE BARD OF ERIN'S LAMENT,	174
THE LAUREATE,	176
A MIDNIGHT MEDITATION,	180
MONTGOMERY: A Poem,	185
THE DEATH OF SPACE,	189
LITTLE JOHN AND THE RED FRIAR: A Lay of Sherwood:—	
Fytte the First,	191
Fytte the Second,	197
THE RHYME OF SIR LAUNCELOT BOGLE: A Legend of Glasgow,	200

MISCELLANEOUS BALLADS—(CONTINUED):—

THE LAY OF THE LOVER'S FRIEND,	223
FRANCESCA DA RIMINI,	227
THE CADI'S DAUGHTER: A LEGEND OF THE BOSPHORUS,	231
THE DIRGE OF THE DRINKER,	236
THE DEATH OF DUVAL,	239
EASTERN SERENADE,	245
DAME FREDEGONDE,	248
THE DEATH OF ISHMAEL,	253
PARR'S LIFE PILLS,	255
TARQUIN AND THE AUGUR,	258
LA MORT D'ARTHUR,	260
JUPITER AND THE INDIAN ALE,	261
THE LAY OF THE DOUDNEY BROTHERS,	264
PARIS AND HELEN,	267
SONG OF THE ENNUYÉ,	270
CAROLINE,	273
TO A FORGET-ME-NOT,	276
THE MISHAP,	278
COMFORT IN AFFLICTION,	281
THE INVOCATION,	283
THE HUSBAND'S PETITION,	287
SONNET TO BRITAIN,	291

L'ENVOY.

Come, buy my lays, and read them if you list;
My pensive public, if you list not, buy.
Come, for you know me. I am he who sang
Of Mister Colt, and I am he who framed
Of Widdicomb the wild and wondrous song.

Come, listen to my lays, and you shall hear
How Wordsworth, battling for the Laureate's wreath,
Bore to the dust the terrible Fitzball;
How N. P. Willis for his country's good,
In complete steel, all bowie-knifed at point,
Took lodgings in the Snapping Turtle's womb.
Come, listen to my lays, and you shall hear
The mingled music of all modern bards
Floating aloft in such peculiar strains,
As strike themselves with envy and amaze;
For you "bright-harped" Tennyson shall sing;
Macaulay chant a more than Roman lay;
And Bulwer Lytton, Lytton Bulwer erst,
Unseen amidst a metaphysic fog,
Howl melancholy homage to the moon;
For you once more Montgomery shall rave
In all his rapt rabidity of rhyme;
Nankeened Cockaigne shall pipe his puny note,
And our young England's penny trumpet blow.

Spanish Ballads

The Broken Pitcher.

It was a Moorish maiden was sitting by a well,
And what the maiden thought of, I cannot, cannot tell,
When by there rode a valiant knight from the town of Oviedo—
Alphonzo Guzman was he hight, the Count of Tolo-ledo.

"Oh, maiden, Moorish maiden, why sit'st thou by
    the spring?
Say, dost thou seek a lover, or any other thing?
Why dost thou look upon me, with eyes so dark and
    wide,
And wherefore doth the pitcher lie broken by thy
    side?"

"I do not seek a lover, thou Christian knight so
    gay,
Because an article like that hath never come my
    way;
And why I gaze upon you, I cannot, cannot tell,
Except that in your iron hose you look uncommon
    swell.

"My pitcher it is broken, and this the reason is,—
A shepherd came behind me, and tried to snatch a
    kiss;
I would not stand his nonsense, so ne'er a word I
    spoke,
But scored him on the costard, and so the jug was
    broke.

"My uncle, the Alcaydè, he waits for me at home,
And will not take his tumbler until Zorayda come:
I cannot bring him water — the pitcher is in
    pieces—
And so I'm sure to catch it, 'cos he wallops all his
    nieces."

"Oh, maiden, Moorish maiden! wilt thou be ruled
    by me?
Then wipe thine eyes and rosy lips, and give me
    kisses three;
And I'll give thee my helmet, thou kind and court-
    eous lady,
To carry home the water to thy uncle, the Alcaydè."

He lighted down from off his steed—he tied him to
    a tree—
He bent him to the maiden, and he took his kisses
    three;
"To wrong thee, sweet Zorayda, I swear would be a
    sin!"
And he knelt him at the fountain, and he dipped his
    helmet in.

Up rose the Moorish maiden—behind the knight she steals,
And caught Alphonzo Guzman in a twinkling by the heels:
She tipped him in, and held him down beneath the bubbling water,—
"Now, take thou that for venturing to kiss Al Hamet's daughter!"

A Christian maid is weeping in the town of Oviedo;
She waits the coming of her love, the Count of Tololedo.
I pray you all in charity, that you will never tell,
How he met the Moorish maiden beside the lonely well.

Don Fernando Gomersalez.

From the Spanish of Astley's.

Don Fernando Gomersalez! basely
 have they borne thee down;
Paces ten behind thy charger is thy
 glorious body thrown;
Fetters have they bound upon thee—
 iron fetters, fast and sure;
Don Fernando Gomersalez, thou art
 captive to the Moor!

Long within a dingy dungeon pined that brave and noble knight,
For the Saracenic warriors well they knew and feared his might;
Long he lay and long he languished on his dripping bed of stone,
Till the cankered iron fetters ate their way into his bone.

On the twentieth day of August—'twas the feast of false Mahound—
Came the Moorish population from the neighbouring cities round;
There to hold their foul carousal, there to dance and there to sing,
And to pay their yearly homage to Al-Widdicomb, the King!

First they wheeled their supple coursers, wheeled them at their utmost speed,
Then they galloped by in squadrons, tossing far the light jereed;

Then around the circus racing, faster than the
  swallow flies,
Did they spurn the yellow sawdust in the rapt
  spectators' eyes.

Proudly did the Moorish monarch every passing
  warrior greet,
As he sate enthroned above them, with the lamps
  beneath his feet;

"Tell me, thou black-bearded Cadi! are there any
    in the land,
That against my janissaries dare one hour in combat
    stand?"

Then the bearded Cadi answered—"Be not wroth,
    my lord the King,
If thy faithful slave shall venture to observe one
    little thing;
Valiant, doubtless, are thy warriors, and their beards
    are long and hairy,
And a thunderbolt in battle is each bristly janissary:

"But I cannot, O my sovereign, quite forget that
    fearful day,
When I saw the Christian army in its terrible
    array;
When they charged across the footlights like a tor-
    rent down its bed,
With the red cross floating o'er them, and Fernando
    at their head!

"Don Fernando Gomersalez! matchless chieftain he
    in war,
Mightier than Don Sticknejo, braver than the Cid
    Bivar!
Not a cheek within Grenada, O my king, but wan
    and pale is,
When they hear the dreaded name of Don Fernando
    Gomersalez!"

"Thou shalt see thy champion, Cadi! hither quick
    the captive bring!"
Thus in wrath and deadly anger spoke Al-Widdi-
    comb, the King:
"Paler than a maiden's forehead is the Christian's
    hue, I ween,
Since a year within the dungeons of Grenada he
    hath been!"

Then they brought the Gomersalez, and they led the
    warrior in;
Weak and wasted seemed his body, and his face was
    pale and thin;

But the ancient fire was burning, unsubdued, within his eye,
And his step was proud and stately, and his look was stern and high.

Scarcely from tumultuous cheering could the galleried crowd refrain,
For they knew Don Gomersalez and his prowess in the plain;
But they feared the grizzly despot and his myrmidons in steel,
So their sympathy descended in the fruitage of Seville.

"Wherefore, monarch, hast thou brought me from the dungeon dark and drear,
Where these limbs of mine have wasted in confinement for a year?
Dost thou lead me forth to torture?—Rack and pincers I defy!
Is it that thy base grotesquos may behold a hero die?"

"Hold thy peace, thou Christian caitiff, and attend
 to what I say!
Thou art called the starkest rider of the Spanish
 cur's array
If thy courage be undaunted, as they say it was of
 yore,
Thou mayst yet achieve thy freedom,—yet regain
 thy native shore.

"Courses three within this circus 'gainst my warriors
 shalt thou run,
Ere yon weltering pasteboard ocean shall receive yon
 muslin sun;
Victor — thou shalt have thy freedom; but if
 stretched upon the plain,
To thy dark and dreary dungeon they shall hale
 thee back again."

"Give me but the armour, monarch, I have worn
 in many a field,
Give me but my trusty helmet, give me but my
 dinted shield;

And my old steed, Bavieca, swiftest courser in the ring,
And I rather should imagine that I'll do the business, King!"

Then they carried down the armour from the garret where it lay,
Oh! but it was red and rusty, and the plumes were shorn away:
And they led out Bavieca from a foul and filthy van,
For the conqueror had sold him to a Moorish dog's-meat man.

When the steed beheld his master, then he whinnied loud and free,
And, in token of subjection, knelt upon each broken knee;
And a tear of walnut largeness to the warrior's eyelids rose,
As he fondly picked a bean-straw from his coughing courser's nose.

"Many a time, O Bavieca, hast thou borne me
    through the fray!
Bear me but again as deftly through the listed
    ring this day;
Or if thou art worn and feeble, as may well have
    come to pass,
Time it is, my trusty charger, both of us were sent
    to grass!"

Then he seized his lance, and, vaulting, in the saddle
    sate upright;
Marble seemed the noble courser, iron seemed the
    mailèd knight;
And a cry of admiration burst from every Moorish
    lady.
"Five to four on Don Fernando!" cried the sable-
    bearded Cadi.

Warriors three from Alcantara burst into the listed
    space,
Warriors three, all bred in battle, of the proud
    Alhambra race:

Trumpets sounded, coursers bounded, and the foremost straight went down,
Tumbling, like a sack of turnips, just before the jeering Clown.

In the second chieftain galloped, and he bowed him to the King,
And his saddle-girths were tightened by the Master of the Ring;
Through three blazing hoops he bounded ere the desperate fight began—
Don Fernando! bear thee bravely!—'tis the Moor Abdorrhaman!

Like a double streak of lightning, clashing in the sulphurous sky,
Met the pair of hostile heroes, and they made the sawdust fly;
And the Moslem spear so stiffly smote on Don Fernando's mail,
That he reeled, as if in liquor, back to Bavieca's tail:

But he caught the mace beside him, and he griped it hard and fast,
And he swung it starkly upwards as the foeman bounded past;
And the deadly stroke descended through the skull and through the brain,
As ye may have seen a poker cleave a cocoa-nut in twain.

Sore astonished was the monarch, and the Moorish warriors all,
Save the third bold chief, who tarried and beheld his brethren fall;
And the Clown, in haste arising from the footstool where he sat,
Notified the first appearance of the famous Acrobat;

Never on a single charger rides that stout and stalwart Moor,—
Five beneath his stride so stately bear him o'er the trembling floor;

Five Arabians, black as midnight—on their necks
    the rein he throws,
And the outer and the inner feel the pressure of
    his toes.

Never wore that chieftain armour; in a knot himself
    he ties,
With his grizzly head appearing in the centre of his
    thighs,
Till the petrified spectator asks, in paralysed alarm,
Where may be the warrior's body,—which is leg,
    and which is arm?

"Sound the charge!" The coursers started; with a
    yell and furious vault,
High in air the Moorish champion cut a wondrous
    somersault;
O'er the head of Don Fernando like a tennis-ball he
    sprung,
Caught him tightly by the girdle, and behind the
    crupper hung.

Then his dagger Don Fernando plucked from out its jewelled sheath,
And he struck the Moor so fiercely, as he grappled him beneath,
That the good Damascus weapon sank within the folds of fat,
And as dead as Julius Cæsar dropped the Gordian Acrobat.

Meanwhile fast the sun was sinking—it had sunk
    beneath the sea,
Ere Fernando Gomersalez smote the latter of the
    three;
And Al-Widdicomb, the monarch, pointed, with a
    bitter smile,
To the deeply-darkening canvas;—blacker grew it
    all the while.

"Thou hast slain my warriors, Spaniard! but thou
    hast not kept thy time;
Only two had sunk before thee ere I heard the cur-
    few chime;
Back thou goest to thy dungeon, and thou may'st be
    wondrous glad,
That thy head is on thy shoulders for thy work to-
    day, my lad!

"Therefore all thy boasted valour, Christian dog, of
    no avail is!"
Dark as midnight grew the brow of Don Fernando
    Gomersalez;—

Stiffly sate he in his saddle, grimly looked around
    the ring,
Laid his lance within the rest, and shook his gaunt-
    let at the King.

"Oh, thou foul and faithless traitor! wouldst thou
    play me false again?
Welcome death and welcome torture, rather than the
    captive's chain!
But I give thee warning, caitiff! Look thou sharply
    to thine eye—
Unavenged, at least in harness, Gomersalez shall not
    die!"

Thus he spoke, and Bavieca like an arrow forward
    flew,
Right and left the Moorish squadron wheeled to let
    the hero through;
Brightly gleamed the lance of vengeance—fiercely
    sped the fatal thrust—
From his throne the Moorish monarch tumbled life-
    less in the dust.

Speed thee, speed thee, Bavieca! speed thee faster than the wind!
Life and freedom are before thee, deadly foes give chase behind!

Speed thee up the sloping spring-board; o'er the
    bridge that spans the seas;
Yonder gauzy moon will light thee through the
    grove of canvas trees.

Close before thee Pampeluna spreads her painted
    pasteboard gate!
Speed thee onward, gallant courser, speed thee with
    thy knightly freight!
Victory! The town receives them!—Gentle ladies,
    this the tale is,
Which I learned in Astley's Circus, of Fernando
    Gomersalez.

The Courtship of our Cid.

WHAT a pang of sweet emotion
    Thrilled the Master of the Ring,
When he first beheld the lady
    Through the stabled portal spring!

Midway in his wild grimacing
  Stopped the piebald-visaged Clown;
And the thunders of the audience
  Nearly brought the gallery down.

Donna Inez Woolfordinez!
  Saw ye ever such a maid,
With the feathers swaling o'er her,
  And her spangled rich brocade?
In her fairy hand a horsewhip,
  On her foot a buskin small,
So she stepped, the stately damsel,
  Through the scarlet grooms and all.

And she beckoned for her courser,
  And they brought a milk-white mare;
Proud, I ween, was that Arabian
  Such a gentle freight to bear:
And the master moved to greet her,
  With a proud and stately walk;
And, in reverential homage,
  Rubbed her soles with virgin chalk.

Round she flew, as Flora flying
  Spans the circle of the year;
And the youth of London, sighing,
  Half forgot the ginger-beer—
Quite forgot the maids beside them;
  As they surely well might do,
When she raised two Roman candles,
  Shooting fireballs red and blue!

Swifter than the Tartar's arrow,
  Lighter than the lark in flight,
On the left foot now she bounded,
  Now she stood upon the right.
Like a beautiful Bacchante,
  Here she soars, and there she kneels,
While amid her floating tresses
  Flash two whirling Catherine wheels!

Hark! the blare of yonder trumpet!
  See, the gates are opened wide!
Room, there, room for Gomersalez,—
  Gomersalez in his pride!

Rose the shouts of exultation,
 Rose the cat's triumphant call,
As he bounded, man and courser,
 Over Master, Clown, and all!

Donna Inez Woolfordinez!
 Why those blushes on thy cheek?
Doth thy trembling bosom tell thee,
 He hath come thy love to seek?
Fleet thy Arab, but behind thee
 He is rushing like a gale;
One foot on his coal-black's shoulders,
 And the other on his tail!

Onward, onward, panting maiden!
 He is faint, and fails, for now
By the feet he hangs suspended
 From his glistening saddle-bow.
Down are gone both cap and feather,
 Lance and gonfalon are down!
Trunks, and cloak, and vest of velvet,
 He has flung them to the Clown.

Faint and failing! Up he vaulteth,
    Fresh as when he first began;
All in coat of bright vermilion,
    'Quipped as Shaw, the Lifeguardsman;
Right and left his whizzing broadsword,
    Like a sturdy flail, he throws;
Cutting out a path unto thee
    Through imaginary foes.

Woolfordinez! speed thee onward!
    He is hard upon thy track,—
Paralysed is Widdicombez,
    Nor his whip can longer crack;
He has flung away his broadsword,
    'Tis to clasp thee to his breast.
Onward!—see, he bares his bosom,
    Tears away his scarlet vest;

Leaps from out his nether garments,
    And his leathern stock unties—
As the flower of London's dustmen,
    Now in swift pursuit he flies.

Nimbly now he cuts and shuffles,
    O'er the buckle, heel and toe!
Flaps his hands in his side-pockets,
    Winks to all the throng below!

Onward, onward rush the coursers;
    Woolfordinez, peerless girl,
O'er the garters lightly bounding
    From her steed with airy whirl!
Gomersalez, wild with passion,
    Danger—all but her—forgets;
Wheresoe'er she flies, pursues her,
    Casting clouds of somersets!

Onward, onward rush the coursers;
    Bright is Gomersalez' eye;
Saints protect thee, Woolfordinez,
    For his triumph sure is nigh!
Now his courser's flanks he lashes,
    O'er his shoulder flings the rein,
And his feet aloft he tosses,
    Holding stoutly by the mane!

Then, his feet once more regaining,
    Doffs his jacket, doffs his smalls,
And in graceful folds around him
    A bespangled tunic falls.
Pinions from his heels are bursting,
    His bright locks have pinions o'er them;
And the public see with rapture
    Maia's nimble son before them.

Speed thee, speed thee, Woolfordinez!
    For a panting god pursues;
And the chalk is very nearly
    Rubbed from thy white satin shoes;
Every bosom throbs with terror,
    You might hear a pin to drop;
All is hushed, save where a starting
    Cork gives out a casual pop.

One smart lash across his courser,
    One tremendous bound and stride,
And our noble Cid was standing
    By his Woolfordinez' side!

THE COURTSHIP OF OUR CID.

With a god's embrace he clasps her,
    Raised her in his manly arms;
And the stables' closing barriers
    Hid his valour, and her charms!

AMERICAN BALLADS

The Fight with the Snapping Turtle;

or,

The American St George.

FYTTE FIRST.

Have you heard of Philip Slingsby,
    Slingsby of the manly chest;
How he slew the Snapping Turtle
    In the regions of the West?

Every day the huge Cawana
    Lifted up its monstrous jaws;
And it swallowed Langton Bennett,
    And digested Rufus Dawes.

Riled, I ween, was Philip Slingsby,
    Their untimely deaths to hear;
For one author owed him money,
    And the other loved him dear.

"Listen now, sagacious Tyler,
    Whom the loafers all obey;
What reward will Congress give me,
    If I take this pest away?"

Then sagacious Tyler answered,
    "You're the ring-tailed squealer! Less
Than a hundred heavy dollars
    Won't be offered you, I guess!

"And a lot of wooden nutmegs
    In the bargain, too, we'll throw—
Only you just fix the critter.
    Won't you liquor ere you go?"

Straightway leaped the valiant Slingsby
    Into armour of Seville,
With a strong Arkansas toothpick
    Screwed in every joint of steel.

"Come thou with me, Cullen Bryant,
  Come with me, as squire, I pray;
Be the Homer of the battle
  Which I go to wage to-day."

So they went along careering
  With a loud and martial tramp,
Till they neared the Snapping Turtle
  In the dreary Swindle Swamp.

But when Slingsby saw the water,
  Somewhat pale, I ween, was he.
"If I come not back, dear Bryant,
  Tell the tale to Melanie!

"Tell her that I died devoted,
  Victim to a noble task!
Han't you got a drop of brandy
  In the bottom of your flask?"

As he spoke, an alligator
  Swam across the sullen creek;
And the two Columbians started,
  When they heard the monster shriek;

For a snout of huge dimensions
    Rose above the waters high,
And took down the alligator,
    As a trout takes down a fly.

"'Tarnal death! the Snapping Turtle!"
    Thus the squire in terror cried;
But the noble Slingsby straightway
    Drew the toothpick from his side.

"Fare thee well!" he cried, and dashing
    Through the waters, strongly swam:
Meanwhile, Cullen Bryant, watching,
    Breathed a prayer and sucked a dram.

Sudden from the slimy bottom
    Was the snout again upreared,
With a snap as loud as thunder,—
    And the Slingsby disappeared.

Like a mighty steam-ship foundering,
    Down the monstrous vision sank;
And the ripple, slowly rolling,
    Plashed and played upon the bank.

Still and stiller grew the water,
    Hushed the canes within the brake;
There was but a kind of coughing
    At the bottom of the lake.

Bryant wept as loud and deeply
    As a father for a son—
"He's a finished 'coon, is Slingsby,
    And the brandy's nearly done!"

FYTTE SECOND.

In a trance of sickening anguish,
    Cold and stiff, and sore and damp,
For two days did Bryant linger
    By the dreary Swindle Swamp;

Always peering at the water,
    Always waiting for the hour
When those monstrous jaws should open
    As he saw them ope before.

Still in vain;—the alligators
    Scrambled through the marshy brake,
And the vampire leeches gaily
    Sucked the garfish in the lake.

But the Snapping Turtle never
    Rose for food or rose for rest,
Since he lodged the steel deposit
    In the bottom of his chest.

Only always from the bottom
    Sounds of frequent coughing rolled,
Just as if the huge Cawana
    Had a most confounded cold.

On the banks lay Cullen Bryant,
    As the second moon arose,
Gouging on the sloping greensward
    Some imaginary foes;

When the swamp began to tremble,
    And the canes to rustle fast,
As though some stupendous body
    Through their roots were crushing past.

And the waters boiled and bubbled,
    And, in groups of twos and threes,
Several alligators bounded,
    Smart as squirrels, up the trees.

Then a hideous head was lifted,
    With such huge distended jaws,
That they might have held Goliath
    Quite as well as Rufus Dawes.

Paws of elephantine thickness
    Dragged its body from the bay,
And it glared at Cullen Bryant
    In a most unpleasant way.

Then it writhed as if in torture,
    And it staggered to and fro;
And its very shell was shaken
    In the anguish of its throe:

And its cough grew loud and louder,
    And its sob more husky thick!
For, indeed, it was apparent
    That the beast was very sick.

42   THE FIGHT WITH THE SNAPPING TURTLE.

Till, at last, a spasmy vomit
    Shook its carcass through and through,
And as if from out a cannon,
    All in armour Slingsby flew.

Bent and bloody was the bowie
    Which he held within his grasp;
And he seemed so much exhausted
    That he scarce had strength to gasp—

"Gouge him, Bryant! darn ye, gouge him!
    Gouge him while he's on the shore!"
Bryant's thumbs were straightway buried
    Where no thumbs had pierced before.

Right from out their bony sockets
    Did he scoop the monstrous balls;
And, with one convulsive shudder,
    Dead the Snapping Turtle falls!

    *   *   *   *

"Post the tin, sagacious Tyler!"
    But the old experienced file,
Leering first at Clay and Webster,
    Answered, with a quiet smile—

44 THE FIGHT WITH THE SNAPPING TURTLE.

"Since you dragged the 'tarnal crittur
From the bottom of the ponds,
Here's the hundred dollars due you,
All in Pennsylvanian Bonds!"

"*The only Good American Securities.*"

The Lay of Mr Colt.

[The story of Mr Colt, of which our Lay contains merely the sequel, is this: A New York printer, of the name of Adams, had the effrontery to call upon him one day for payment of an account, which the independent Colt settled by cutting his creditor's head to fragments with an axe. He then packed his body in a box, and sprinkling it with salt, despatched it to a packet bound for New Orleans. Suspicions having been excited, he was seized and tried before Judge Kent. The trial is, perhaps, the most disgraceful upon the records of any country. The ruffian's mistress was produced in court, and examined, in disgusting detail, as to her connection with Colt, and his movements during the days and nights succeeding the murder. The head of the murdered man was handied to and fro in the court, handed up to the jury, and commented on by witnesses and counsel; and to crown the horrors of the whole proceeding, the wretch's own counsel, a Mr Emmet, commencing the defence with a cool admission that his client took the life of Adams, and following it up by a detail of the whole circumstances of this most brutal murder in the first person, as though he himself had been the murderer, ended by telling the jury, that his client was "*entitled to the sympathy* of a jury of his country," as "a young man just entering into life, *whose prospects, probably, have been permanently blasted.*" Colt was found guilty; but a variety of exceptions were taken to the charge by the judge, and after a long series of appeals, which *occupied more than a year from the date of conviction*, the sentence of death was ratified by Governor Seward. The rest of Colt's story is told in our ballad.]

STREAK THE FIRST.

*   *   *   *

AND now the sacred rite was done, and the marriage-
    knot was tied,
And Colt withdrew his blushing wife a little way
    aside;

"Let's go," he said, "into my cell; let's go alone, my dear;
I fain would shelter that sweet face from the sheriff's odious leer.
The jailer and the hangman, they are waiting both for me,—
I cannot bear to see them wink so knowingly at thee!
Oh, how I loved thee, dearest! They say that I am wild,
That a mother dares not trust me with the weasand of her child;
They say my bowie-knife is keen to sliver into halves
The carcass of my enemy, as butchers slay their calves.
They say that I am stern of mood, because, like salted beef,
I packed my quartered foeman up, and marked him 'prime tariff;'
Because I thought to palm him on the simple-souled John Bull,
And clear a small percentage on the sale at Liverpool;
It may be so, I do not know—these things, perhaps, may be;
But surely I have always been a gentleman to thee!

Then come, my love, into my cell, short bridal space
    is ours,—
Nay, sheriff, never con thy watch—I guess there's
    good two hours.
We'll shut the prison doors and keep the gaping
    world at bay,
For love is long as 'tarnity, though I must die to-
    day!"

STREAK THE SECOND.

The clock is ticking onward,
    It nears the hour of doom,
And no one yet hath entered
    Into that ghastly room.
The jailer and the sheriff,
    They are walking to and fro:
And the hangman sits upon the steps,
    And smokes his pipe below.
In grisly expectation
    The prison all is bound,
And, save expectoration,
    You cannot hear a sound.

The turnkey stands and ponders,—
    His hand upon the bolt,—
" In twenty minutes more, I guess,
    'Twill all be up with Colt!"
But see, the door is opened!
    Forth comes the weeping bride;
The courteous sheriff lifts his hat,
    And saunters to her side,—
" I beg your pardon, Mrs C.,
    But is your husband ready?"
" I guess you'd better ask himself,"
    Replied the woeful lady.

The clock is ticking onward,
    The minutes almost run,
The hangman's pipe is nearly out,
    'Tis on the stroke of one.
At every grated window,
    Unshaven faces glare;
There's Puke, the judge of Tennessee,
    And Lynch, of Delaware;
And Batter, with the long black beard,
    Whom Hartford's maids know well;

And Winkinson, from Fish Kill Reach,
 The pride of New Rochelle;
Elkanah Nutts, from Tarry Town,
 The gallant gouging boy;
And 'coon-faced Bushwhack, from the hills
 That frown o'er modern Troy;
Young Julep, whom our Willis loves,
 Because, 'tis said, that he
One morning from a bookstall filched
 The tale of "Melanie;"
And Skunk, who fought his country's fight
 Beneath the stripes and stars,—
All thronging at the windows stood,
 And gazed between the bars.
The little boys that stood behind
 (Young thievish imps were they!)
Displayed considerable *nous*
 On that eventful day;
For bits of broken looking-glass
 They held aslant on high,
And there a mirrored gallows-tree
 Met their delighted eye.[1]

[1] A fact.

The clock is ticking onward;
    Hark! hark! it striketh one!
Each felon draws a whistling breath,
    "Time's up with Colt! he's done!"

The sheriff cons his watch again,
    Then puts it in his fob,
And turning to the hangman, says,—
    "Get ready for the job."
The jailer knocketh loudly,
    The turnkey draws the bolt,
And pleasantly the sheriff says,
    "We're waiting, Mister Colt!"

No answer! no! no answer!
    All's still as death within;
The sheriff eyes the jailer,
    The jailer strokes his chin.
"I shouldn't wonder, Nahum, if
    It were as you suppose."
The hangman looked unhappy, and
    The turnkey blew his nose.

They entered. On his pallet
    The noble convict lay,—
The bridegroom on his marriage-bed
    But not in trim array.
His red right hand a razor held,
    Fresh sharpened from the hone,
And his ivory neck was severed,
    And gashed into the bone.

    *   *   *   *

And when the lamp is lighted
    In the long November days,
And lads and lasses mingle
    At the shucking of the maize;
When pies of smoking pumpkin
    Upon the table stand,
And bowls of black molasses
    Go round from hand to hand;
When slap-jacks, maple-sugared,
    Are hissing in the pan,
And cider, with a dash of gin,
    Foams in the social can;

When the goodman wets his whistle,
    And the goodwife scolds the child;
And the girls exclaim convulsively,
    "Have done, or I'll be riled!"
When the loafer sitting next them
    Attempts a sly caress,
And whispers, "Oh, you 'possum,
    You've fixed my heart, I guess!"
With laughter and with weeping,
    Then shall they tell the tale,
How Colt his foeman quartered,
    And died within the jail.

"*The Unwilling Colt.*"

The Death of Jabez Dollar.

[Before the following poem, which originally appeared in 'Fraser's Magazine,' could have reached America, intelligence was received in this country of an affray in Congress, very nearly the counterpart of that which the Author has here imagined in jest. It was very clear, to any one who observed the state of public manners at that time in America, that such occurrences *must* happen, sooner or later. The Americans apparently felt the force of the satire, as the poem was widely reprinted throughout the States. It subsequently returned to this country, embodied in an American work on American manners, where it characteristically appeared as the writer's *own* production; and it afterwards went the round of British newspapers, as an amusing satire, by an American, of his countrymen's foibles!]

The Congress met, the day was wet, Van Buren took the chair;
On either side, the statesman pride of far Kentuck was there.
With moody frown, there sat Calhoun, and slowly in his cheek
His quid he thrust, and slaked the dust, as Webster rose to speak.

Upon that day, near gifted Clay, a youthful member sat,
And like a free American upon the floor he spat;

Then turning round to Clay, he said, and wiped his
 manly chin,
"What kind of Locofoco's that, as wears the painter's
 skin?"

"Young man," quoth Clay, "avoid the way of Slick
 of Tennessee;
Of gougers fierce, the eyes that pierce, the fiercest
 gouger he;
He chews and spits, as there he sits, and whittles at
 the chairs,
And in his hand, for deadly strife, a bowie-knife he
 bears.

"Avoid that knife. In frequent strife its blade, so
 long and thin,
Has found itself a resting-place his rivals' ribs
 within."
But coward fear came never near young Jabez Dollar's
 heart,—
"Were he an alligator, I would rile him pretty
 smart!"

Then up he rose, and cleared his nose, and looked
    toward the chair;
He saw the stately stripes and stars,—our country's
    flag was there!
His heart beat high, with eldritch cry upon the floor
    he sprang,
Then raised his wrist, and shook his fist, and spoke
    his first harangue.

"Who sold the nutmegs made of wood—the clocks
    that wouldn't figure?
Who grinned the bark off gum-trees dark—the ever-
    lasting nigger?
For twenty cents, ye Congress gents, through 'tarnity
    I'll kick
That man, I guess, though nothing less than 'coon-
    faced Colonel Slick!"

The Colonel smiled—with frenzy wild,—his very
    beard waxed blue,—
His shirt it could not hold him, so wrathy riled he
    grew;

He foams and frets, his knife he whets upon his seat below—
He sharpens it on either side, and whittles at his toe.

"Oh! waken snakes, and walk your chalks!" he cried, with ire elate;
"Darn my old mother, but I will in wild cats whip my weight!
Oh! 'tarnal death, I'll spoil your breath, young Dollar, and your chaffing,—
Look to your ribs, for here is that will tickle them without laughing!"

His knife he raised—with fury crazed, he sprang across the hall;
He cut a caper in the air—he stood before them all:
He never stopped to look or think if he the deed should do,
But spinning sent the President, and on young Dollar flew.

They met—they closed—they sank—they rose,—in
    vain young Dollar strove—
For, like a streak of lightning greased, the infuriate
    Colonel drove
His bowie-blade deep in his side, and to the ground
    they rolled,
And, drenched in gore, wheeled o'er and o'er, locked
    in each other's hold.

With fury dumb—with nail and thumb—they strug-
    gled and they thrust,—
The blood ran red from Dollar's side, like rain, upon
    the dust;
He nerved his might for one last spring, and as he
    sank and died,
Reft of an eye, his enemy fell groaning by his side.

Thus did he fall within the hall of Congress, that
    brave youth;
The bowie-knife has quenched his life of valour and
    of truth;

And still among the statesmen throng at Washington
    they tell
How nobly Dollar gouged his man—how gallantly
    he fell.

The Alabama Duel.

"Young chaps, give ear, the case is clear. You,
 Silas Fixings, you
Pay Mister Nehemiah Dodge them dollars as you're
 due.

You are a bloody cheat,—you are. But spite of all
    your tricks, it
Is not in you Judge Lynch to do. No! nohow you
    can fix it!"

Thus spake Judge Lynch, as there he sat in Alabama's
    forum,
Around he gazed, with legs upraised upon the bench
    before him;
And, as he gave this sentence stern to him who stood
    beneath,
Still with his gleaming bowie-knife he slowly picked
    his teeth.

It was high noon, the month was June, and sultry
    was the air,
A cool gin-sling stood by his hand, his coat hung
    o'er his chair;
All naked were his manly arms, and shaded by his
    hat,
Like an old senator of Rome that simple Archon sat.

"A bloody cheat?—Oh, legs and feet!" in wrath
    young Silas cried;
And springing high into the air, he jerked his quid
    aside.
"No man shall put my dander up, or with my feel-
    ings trifle,
As long as Silas Fixings wears a bowie-knife and
    rifle."

"If your shoes pinch," replied Judge Lynch, "you'll
    very soon have ease;
I'll give you satisfaction, squire, in any way you
    please;
What are your weapons?—knife or gun?—at both
    I'm pretty spry!"
"Oh! 'tarnal death, you're spry, you are?" quoth
    Silas; "so am I!"

Hard by the town a forest stands, dark with the
    shades of time,
And they have sought that forest dark at morning's
    early prime.

Lynch, backed by Nehemiah Dodge, and Silas with
    a friend,
And half the town in glee came down to see that
    contest's end.

They led their men two miles apart, they measured
    out the ground;
A belt of that vast wood it was, they notched the
    trees around;
Into the tangled brake they turned them off, and
    neither knew
Where he should seek his wagered foe, how get him
    into view.

With stealthy tread, and stooping head, from tree
    to tree they passed,
They crept beneath the crackling furze, they held
    their rifles fast:
Hour passed on hour, the noonday sun smote fiercely
    down, but yet
No sound to the expectant crowd proclaimed that
    they had met.

And now the sun was going down, when, hark! a rifle's crack!
Hush—hush! another strikes the air,— and all their breath draw back,—
Then crashing on through bush and briar, the crowd from either side
Rush in to see whose rifle sure with blood the moss has dyed.

Weary with watching up and down, brave Lynch conceived a plan,
An artful dodge whereby to take at unawares his man;

He hung his hat upon a bush, and hid himself hard by;
Young Silas thought he had him fast, and at the hat let fly.

It fell; up sprang young Silas,—he hurled his gun away;
Lynch fixed him with his rifle, from the ambush where he lay.
The bullet pierced his manly breast—yet, valiant to the last,
Young Fixings drew his bowie-knife, and up his foxtail[1] cast.

With tottering step and glazing eye he cleared the space between,
And stabbed the air as stabs in grim Macbeth the younger Kean:
Brave Lynch received him with a bang that stretched him on the ground,
Then sat himself serenely down till all the crowd drew round.

[1] The Yankee substitute for the *chapeau de soie*.

They hailed him with triumphant cheers—in him
    each loafer saw
The bearing bold that could uphold the majesty of
    law;
And, raising him aloft, they bore him homewards at
    his ease,—
That noble judge, whose daring hand enforced his
    own decrees.

They buried Silas Fixings in the hollow where
    he fell,
And gum-trees wave above his grave—that tree he
    loved so well;
And the 'coons sit chattering o'er him when the
    nights are long and damp;
But he sleeps well in that lonely dell, the Dreary
    'Possum Swamp.

The American's Apostrophe to Boz.

[So rapidly does oblivion do its work nowadays, that the burst of indignation with which America received the issue of Boz's *American Notes* is now all but forgotten. Not content with waging a universal rivalry in the piracy of the work, Columbia showered upon its author the riches of its own copious vocabulary of abuse; while some of her more fiery spirits threw out playful hints as to the propriety of gouging the "stranger," and furnishing him with a permanent suit of tar and feathers, in the then very improbable event of his paying them a second visit. The perusal of these animated expressions of free opinion suggested the following lines, at a time when the press was full of notices of Boz's book, and the festivities with which he was all but hunted to death when in America, were fresh in everybody's remembrance. The American people and their critic subsequently came to understand each other better.]

SNEAK across the wide Atlantic, worthless London's
    puling child,
Better that its waves should bear thee, than the
    land thou hast reviled;
Better in the stifling cabin, on the sofa thou
    shouldst lie,
Sickening as the fetid nigger bears the greens and
    bacon by;

Better, when the midnight horrors haunt the strained
    and creaking ship,
Thou shouldst yell in vain for brandy with a fever-
    sodden lip;
When amid the deepening darkness and the lamp's
    expiring shade,
From the bagman's berth above thee comes the
    bountiful cascade,
Better than upon the Broadway thou shouldst be at
    noonday seen,
Smirking like a Tracy Tupman with a Mantalini mien,
With a rivulet of satin falling o'er thy puny chest,
Worse than even N. P. Willis for an evening party
    drest!

We received thee warmly — kindly — though we
    knew thou wert a quiz,
Partly for thyself it may be, chiefly for the sake of
    Phiz!
Much we bore, and much we suffered, listening to
    remorseless spells
Of that Smike's unceasing drivellings, and these
    everlasting Nells.

When you talked of babes and sunshine, fields, and
    all that sort of thing,
Each Columbian inly chuckled, as he slowly sucked
    his sling;
And though all our sleeves were bursting, from the
    many hundreds near
Not one single scornful titter rose on thy complacent
    ear.
Then to show thee to the ladies, with our usual want
    of sense
We engaged the place in Park Street at a ruinous
    expense;
Even our own three-volumed Cooper waived his old
    prescriptive right,
And deluded Dickens figured first on that eventful
    night.
Clusters of uncoated Yorkers, vainly striving to be
    cool,
Saw thee desperately plunging through the perils of
    La Poule:
And their muttered exclamation drowned the tenor
    of the tune,—
    Don't he beat all natur hollow? Don't he foot it
        like a 'coon?"

Did we spare our brandy-cocktails, stint thee of our whisky-grogs?
Half the juleps that we gave thee would have floored a Newman Noggs;
And thou took'st them in so kindly, little was there then to blame,
To thy parched and panting palate sweet as mother's milk they came.
Did the hams of old Virginny find no favour in thine eyes?
Came no soft compunction o'er thee at the thought of pumpkin pies?
Could not all our chicken fixings into silence fix thy scorn?
Did not all our cakes rebuke thee,—Johnny, waffle, dander, corn?
Could not all our care and coddling teach thee how to draw it mild?
Well, no matter, we deserve it. Serves us right! We spoilt the child!

You, forsooth, must come crusading, boring us with broadest hints
Of your own peculiar losses by American reprints.

Such an impudent remonstrance never in our face
    was flung;
Lever stands it, so does Ainsworth; *you*, I guess,
    may hold your tongue.
Down our throats you'd cram your projects, thick
    and hard as pickled salmon,
That, I s'pose, you call free trading,— I pronounce it
    utter gammon.
No, my lad, a 'cuter vision than your own might
    soon have seen,
That a true Columbian ogle carries little that is green;
That we never will surrender useful privateering
    rights,
Stoutly won at glorious Bunker's Hill, and other
    famous fights;
That we keep our native dollars for our native
    scribbling gents,
And on British manufacture only waste our strag-
    gling cents;
Quite enough we pay, I reckon, when we stump of
    these a few
For the voyages and travels of a freshman such as
    you.

I have been at Niagara, I have stood beneath the
    Falls,
I have marked the water twisting over its rampagious
    walls;
But "a holy calm sensation," one, in fact, of perfect
    peace,
Was as much my first idea as the thought of
    Christmas geese.
As for "old familiar faces," looking through the
    misty air,
Surely you were strongly liquored when you saw
    your Chuckster there.
One familiar face, however, you will very likely see,
If you'll only treat the natives to a call in Tennessee,
Of a certain individual, true Columbian every inch,
In a high judicial station, called by 'mancipators,
    Lynch.
Half an hour of conversation with his worship in a
    wood,
Would, I strongly notion, do you an infernal deal of
    good.
Then you'd understand more clearly than you ever
    did before,

Why an independent patriot freely spits upon the
   floor,
Why he gouges when he pleases, why he whittles at
   the chairs,
Why for swift and deadly combat still the bowie-
   knife he bears,—
Why he sneers at the old country with republican
   disdain,
And, unheedful of the negro's cry, still tighter draws
   his chain.
All these things the judge shall teach thee of the
   land thou hast reviled;
Get thee o'er the wide Atlantic, worthless London's
   puling child!

MISCELLANEOUS BALLADS

The Student of Jena.

ONCE—'twas when I lived at Jena—
    At a Wirthshaus' door I sat;
And in pensive contemplation
    Ate the sausage thick and fat;
Ate the kraut that never sourer
    Tasted to my lips than here;
Smoked my pipe of strong canaster,
    Sipped my fifteenth jug of beer;
Gazed upon the glancing river,
    Gazed upon the tranquil pool,

Whence the silver-voiced Undine,
    When the nights were calm and cool,
As the Baron Fouqué tells us,
    Rose from out her shelly grot,
Casting glamour o'er the waters,
    Witching that enchanted spot.
From the shadow which the coppice
    Flings across the rippling stream,
Did I hear a sound of music—
    Was it thought or was it dream?
There, beside a pile of linen,
    Stretched along the daisied sward,
Stood a young and blooming maiden—
    'Twas her thrush-like song I heard.
Evermore within the eddy
    Did she plunge the white chemise;
And her robes were loosely gathered
    Rather far above her knees;
Then my breath at once forsook me,
    For too surely did I deem
That I saw the fair Undine
    Standing in the glancing stream—
And I felt the charm of knighthood;

And from that remembered day,
Every evening to the Wirthshaus
  Took I my enchanted way.

Shortly to relate my story,
  Many a week of summer long
Came I there, when beer-o'ertaken,
  With my lute and with my song;
Sang in mellow-toned soprano
  All my love and all my woe,
Till the river-maiden answered,
  Lilting in the stream below:—
"Fair Undine! sweet Undine!
  Dost thou love as I love thee?"
"Love is free as running water,"
  Was the answer made to me.

Thus, in interchange seraphic,
  Did I woo my phantom fay,
Till the nights grew long and chilly,
  Short and shorter grew the day;
Till at last—'twas dark and gloomy,
  Dull and starless was the sky,

And my steps were all unsteady
    For a little flushed was I,—
To the well-accustomed signal
    No response the maiden gave;
But I heard the waters washing
    And the moaning of the wave.
Vanished was my own Undine,
    All her linen, too, was gone;
And I walked about lamenting
    On the river bank alone.
Idiot that I was, for never
    Had I asked the maiden's name.
Was it Lieschen—was it Gretchen?
    Had she tin, or whence she came?
So I took my trusty meerschaum,
    And I took my lute likewise;
Wandered forth in minstrel fashion,
    Underneath the louring skies;
Sang before each comely Wirthshaus,
    Sang beside each purling stream,
That same ditty which I chanted
    When Undine was my theme,
Singing, as I sang at Jena,

When the shifts were hung to dry,
"Fair Undine! young Undine!
Dost thou love as well as I?"

But, alas! in field or village,
　Or beside the pebbly shore,
Did I see those glancing ankles,
　And the white robe never more;
And no answer came to greet me,
　No sweet voice to mine replied;
But I heard the waters rippling,
　And the moaning of the tide.

"*The moaning of the* TIED."

The Lay of the Levite.

THERE is a sound that's dear to me,
    It haunts me in my sleep;
I wake, and, if I hear it not,
    I cannot choose but weep.
Above the roaring of the wind,
    Above the river's flow,
Methinks I hear the mystic cry
    Of "Clo!—Old Clo!"

The exile's song, it thrills among
    The dwellings of the free,

Its sound is strange to English ears,
  But 'tis not strange to me;
For it hath shook the tented field
  In ages long ago,
And hosts have quailed before the cry
  Of "Clo!—Old Clo!"

Oh, lose it not! forsake it not!
  And let no time efface
The memory of that solemn sound,
  The watchword of our race;
For not by dark and eagle eye
  The Hebrew shall you know,
So well as by the plaintive cry
  Of "Clo!—Old Clo!"

Even now, perchance, by Jordan's banks,
  Or Sidon's sunny walls,
Where, dial-like, to portion time,
  The palm-tree's shadow falls,
The pilgrims, wending on their way,
  Will linger as they go,
And listen to the distant cry
  Of "Clo!—Old Clo!"

Bursch Groggenburg.

[AFTER THE MANNER OF SCHILLER.]

"Bursch! if foaming beer content ye,
  Come and drink your fill;
In our cellars there is plenty;
  Himmel! how you swill!
That the liquor hath allurance,
  Well I understand;
But 'tis really past endurance,
  When you squeeze my hand!"

And he heard her as if dreaming,
    Heard her half in awe;
And the meerschaum's smoke came streaming
    From his open jaw:
And his pulse beat somewhat quicker
    Than it did before,
And he finished off his liquor,
    Staggered through the door;

Bolted off direct to Munich,
    And within the year
Underneath his German tunic
    Stowed whole butts of beer.
And he drank like fifty fishes,
    Drank till all was blue;
For he felt extremely vicious—
    Somewhat thirsty too.

But at length this dire deboshing
    Drew towards an end;
Few of all his silver groschen
    Had he left to spend.

And he knew it was not prudent
  Longer to remain;
So, with weary feet, the student
  Wended home again.

At the tavern's well-known portal
  Knocks he as before,
And a waiter, rather mortal,
  Hiccups through the door—
"Master's sleeping in the kitchen;
  You'll alarm the house;
Yesterday the Jungfrau Fritchen
  Married baker Kraus!"

Like a fiery comet bristling,
  Rose the young man's hair,
And, poor soul! he fell a-whistling
  Out of sheer despair.
Down the gloomy street in silence,
  Savage-calm he goes;
But he did no deed of vi'lence—
  Only blew his nose.

Then he hired an airy garret
  Near her dwelling-place;
Grew a beard of fiercest carrot,
  Never washed his face;
Sate all day beside the casement,
  Sate a dreary man;
Found in smoking such an easement
  As the wretched can;

Stared for hours and hours together,
  Stared yet more and more;
Till in fine and sunny weather,
  At the baker's door,
Stood, in apron white and mealy,
  That belovèd dame,
Counting out the loaves so freely,
  Selling of the same.

Then like a volcano puffing,
  Smoked he out his pipe;
Sighed and supped on ducks and stuffing,
  Ham and kraut and tripe;

Went to bed, and, in the morning,
    Waited as before,
Still his eyes in anguish turning
    To the baker's door;

Till, with apron white and mealy,
    Came the lovely dame,
Counting out the loaves so freely,
    Selling of the same.
So one day—the fact's amazing!—
    On his post he died!
And they found the body gazing
    At the baker's bride.

Night and Morning.

[NOT BY SIR E. BULWER LYTTON.]

"Thy coffee, Tom, 's untasted,
    And thy egg is very cold;
Thy cheeks are wan and wasted,
    Not rosy as of old.
My boy, what has come o'er ye?
    You surely are not well!
Try some of that ham before ye,
    And then, Tom, ring the bell!"

"I cannot eat, my mother,
    My tongue is parched and bound,
And my head, somehow or other,
    Is swimming round and round.

In my eyes there is a fulness,
    And my pulse is beating quick;
On my brain is a weight of dulness:
    Oh, mother, I am sick!"

"These long, long nights of watching
    Are killing you outright;
The evening dews are catching,
    And you're out every night.
Why does that horrid grumbler,
    Old Inkpen, work you so?"

(Tom—*lene susurrans*)

"My head! Oh, that tenth tumbler!
    'Twas that which wrought my woe!"

The Biter Bit.

The sun is in the sky, mother, the flowers are springing fair,
And the melody of woodland birds is stirring in the air;
The river, smiling to the sky, glides onward to the sea,
And happiness is everywhere, oh mother, but with me!

They are going to the church, mother,—I hear the marriage-bell;
It booms along the upland,—oh! it haunts me like a knell;
He leads her on his arm, mother, he cheers her faltering step,
And closely to his side she clings,—she does, the demirep!

They are crossing by the stile, mother, where we so oft have stood,
The stile beside the shady thorn, at the corner of the wood;

And the boughs, that wont to murmur back the
    words that won my ear,
Wave their silver blossoms o'er him, as he leads his
    bridal fere.

He will pass beside the stream, mother, where first
    my hand he pressed,
By the meadow where, with quivering lip, his passion
    he confessed;
And down the hedgerows where we've strayed again
    and yet again;
But he will not think of me, mother, his broken-
    hearted Jane!

He said that I was proud, mother,—that I looked
    for rank and gold;
He said I did not love him,—he said my words were
    cold;
He said I kept him off and on, in hopes of higher
    game,—
And it may be that I did, mother; but who hasn't
    done the same?

I did not know my heart, mother,—I know it now
    too late;

I thought that I without a pang could wed some
    nobler mate;
But no nobler suitor sought me,—and he has taken
    wing,
And my heart is gone, and I am left a lone and
    blighted thing.

You may lay me in my bed, mother,—my head is
    throbbing sore;
And, mother, prithee, let the sheets be duly aired
    before;
And, if you'd do a kindness to your poor desponding
    child,
Draw me a pot of beer, mother—and, mother, draw
    it mild!

"*Love gone to pot.*"

The Meeting.

Once I lay beside a fountain,
    Lulled me with its gentle song,
And my thoughts o'er dale and mountain
    With the clouds were borne along.

There I saw old castles flinging
    Shadowy gleams on moveless seas,
Saw gigantic forests swinging
    To and fro without a breeze;

And in dusky alleys straying,
    Many a giant shape of power,
Troops of nymphs in sunshine playing,
    Singing, dancing, hour on hour.

I, too, trod these plains Elysian,
    Heard their ringing tones of mirth,
But a brighter, fairer vision
    Called me back again to earth.

THE MEETING.

From the forest shade advancing,
    See, where comes a lovely May;
The dew, like gems, before her glancing,
    As she brushes it away!

Straight I rose, and ran to meet her,
    Seized her hand—the heavenly blue
Of her eyes smiled brighter, sweeter,
    As she asked me—"Who are you?"

To that question came another—
    What its aim I still must doubt—
And she asked me, "How's your mother?
    Does she know that you are out?"

"No! my mother does not know it,
    Beauteous, heaven-descended muse!"
"Then be off, my handsome poet,
    And say I sent you with the news!"

The Convict and the Australian Lady.

Thy skin is dark as jet, ladye,
    Thy cheek is sharp and high,
And there's a cruel leer, love,
    Within thy rolling eye:

These tangled ebon tresses
    No comb hath e'er gone through;
And thy forehead, it is furrowed by
    The elegant tattoo!

I love thee,—oh, I love thee,
    Thou strangely-feeding maid!
Nay, lift not thus thy boomerang,
    I meant not to upbraid!
Come, let me taste those yellow lips
    That ne'er were tasted yet,
Save when the shipwrecked mariner
    Passed through them for a whet.

Nay, squeeze me not so tightly!
    For I am gaunt and thin;
There's little flesh to tempt thee
    Beneath a convict's skin.
I came not to be eaten;
    I sought thee, love, to woo;
Besides, bethink thee, dearest,
    Thou'st dined on cockatoo.

Thy father is a chieftain!
 Why, that's the very thing!
Within my native country
 I too have been a king.
Behold this branded letter,
 Which nothing can efface!
It is the royal emblem,
 The token of my race!

But rebels rose against me,
 And dared my power disown—
You've heard, love, of the judges?
 They drove me from my throne.
And I have wandered hither,
 Across the stormy sea,
In search of glorious freedom,—
 In search, my sweet, of thee!

The bush is now my empire,
 The knife my sceptre keen;
Come with me to the desert wild,
 And be my dusky queen.

I cannot give thee jewels,
    I have nor sheep nor cow,
Yet there are kangaroos, love,
    And colonists enow.

We'll meet the unwary settler,
    As whistling home he goes,
And I'll take tribute from him,
    His money and his clothes.
Then on his bleeding carcass
    Thou'lt lay thy pretty paw,
And lunch upon him roasted,
    Or, if you like it, raw!

Then come with me, my princess,
    My own Australian dear,
Within this grove of gum-trees
    We'll hold our bridal cheer!
Thy heart with love is beating,
    I feel it through my side:—
Hurrah, then, for the noble pair,
    The Convict and his Bride!

The Doleful Lay of the Honourable I. O. Uwins.

Come and listen, lords and ladies,
    To a woeful lay of mine;
He whose tailor's bill unpaid is,
    Let him now his ear incline!
Let him hearken to my story,
    How the noblest of the land
Pined in piteous purgatory,
    'Neath a sponging Bailiff's hand.

I. O. Uwins! I. O. Uwins!
    Baron's son although thou be,
Thou must pay for thy misdoings
    In the country of the free!
None of all thy sire's retainers
    To thy rescue now may come;
And there lie some score detainers
    With Abednego, the bum.

Little recked he of his prison
    Whilst the sun was in the sky:
Only when the moon was risen
    Did you hear the captive's cry.
For till then, cigars and claret
    Lulled him in oblivion sweet;
And he much preferred a garret,
    For his drinking, to the street.

But the moonlight, pale and broken,
    Pained at soul the baron's son;
For he knew, by that soft token,
    That the larking had begun;—
That the stout and valiant Marquis
    Then was leading forth his swells,
Milling some policeman's carcass,
    Or purloining private bells.

So he sat in grief and sorrow,
    Rather drunk than otherwise,
Till the golden gush of morrow
    Dawned once more upon his eyes:

Till the sponging Bailiff's daughter,
    Lightly tapping at the door,
Brought his draught of soda-water,
    Brandy-bottomed as before.

"Sweet Rebecca! has your father,
    Think you, made a deal of brass?"
And she answered—"Sir, I rather
    Should imagine that he has."
Uwins then, his whiskers scratching,
    Leered upon the maiden's face,
And, her hand with ardour catching,
    Folded her in close embrace.

"La, Sir! let alone—you fright me!"
    Said the daughter of the Jew:
"Dearest, how those eyes delight me!
    Let me love thee, darling, do!"
"Vat is dish?" the Bailiff muttered,
    Rushing in with fury wild;
"Ish your muffins so vell buttered,
    Dat you darsh insult ma shild?"

"Honourable my intentions,
  Good Abednego, I swear!
And I have some small pretensions,
  For I am a Baron's heir.
If you'll only clear my credit,
  And advance a *thou*[1] or so,
She's a peeress—I have said it:
  Don't you twig, Abednego?"

"Datsh a very different matter,"
  Said the Bailiff, with a leer;
"But you musht not cut it fatter
  Than ta slish will shtand, ma tear!
If you seeksh ma approbation,
  You musht quite give up your rigsh,
Alsho you musht join our nashun,
  And renounsh ta flesh of pigsh."

Fast as one of Fagin's pupils,
  I. O. Uwins did agree!
Little plagued with holy scruples
  From the starting-post was he.

[1] The fashionable abbreviation for a thousand pounds.

But at times a baleful vision
    Rose before his shuddering view,
For he knew that circumcision
    Was expected from a Jew.

At a meeting of the Rabbis,
    Held about the Whitsuntide,
Was this thorough-paced Barabbas
    Wedded to his Hebrew bride:
All his previous debts compounded,
    From the sponging-house he came,
And his father's feelings wounded
    With reflections on the same.

But the sire his son accosted—
    "Split my wig! if any more
Such a double-dyed apostate
    Shall presume to cross my door!
Not a penny-piece to save ye
    From the kennel or the spout;—
Dinner, John! the pig and gravy!—
    Kick this dirty scoundrel out!"

Forth rushed I. O. Uwins, faster
    Than all winking—much afraid

That the orders of the master
    Would be punctually obeyed:
Sought his club, and then the sentence
    Of expulsion first he saw;
No one dared to own acquaintance
    With a Bailiff's son-in-law.

Uselessly, down Bond Street strutting,
    Did he greet his friends of yore:
Such a universal cutting
    Never man received before:
Till at last his pride revolted—
    Pale, and lean, and stern he grew;
And his wife Rebecca bolted
    With a missionary Jew.

Ye who read this doleful ditty,
    Ask ye where is Uwins now?
Wend your way through London city,
    Climb to Holborn's lofty brow;
Near the sign-post of the "Nigger,"
    Near the baked-potato shed,
You may see a ghastly figure
    With three hats upon his head.

When the evening shades are dusky,
　　Then the phantom form draws near,
And, with accents low and husky,
　　Pours effluvium in your ear;
Craving an immediate barter
　　Of your trousers or surtout;
And you know the Hebrew martyr,
　　Once the peerless I. O. U.

The Knyghte and the Taylzeour's Daughter.

Did you ever hear the story—
  Old the legend is, and true—
How a knyghte of fame and glory
  All aside his armour threw;

Spouted spear and pawned habergeon,
    Pledged his sword and surcoat gay,
Sate down cross-legged on the shop-board,
    Sate and stitched the livelong day?

"Taylzeour! not one single shilling
    Does my breeches-pocket hold:
I to pay am really willing,
    If I only had the gold.
Farmers none can I encounter,
    Graziers there are none to kill;
Therefore, prithee, gentle taylzeour,
    Bother not about thy bill."

"Good Sir Knyghte, just once too often
    Have you tried that slippery trick;
Hearts like mine you cannot soften,
    Vainly do you ask for tick.
Christmas and its bills are coming,
    Soon will they be showering in;
Therefore, once for all, my rum un,
    I expect you'll post the tin.

"Mark, Sir Knyghte, that gloomy bayliffe
    In the palmer's amice brown;
He shall lead you unto jail, if
    Instantly you stump not down."
Deeply swore the young crusader,
    But the taylzeour would not hear;
And the gloomy, bearded bayliffe
    Evermore kept sneaking near.

"Neither groat nor maravedi
    Have I got my soul to bless;
And I'd feel extremely seedy,
    Languishing in vile duresse.
Therefore listen, ruthless taylzeour,
    Take my steed and armour free,
Pawn them at thy Hebrew uncle's,
    And I'll work the rest for thee."

Lightly leaped he on the shop-board,
    Lightly crooked his manly limb,
Lightly drove the glancing needle
    Through the growing doublet's rim.

Gaberdines in countless number
　　Did the taylzeour knyghte repair,
And entirely on cucumber
　　And on cabbage lived he there.

Once his weary task beguiling
　　With a low and plaintive song,
That good knyghte o'er miles of broadcloth
　　Drove the hissing goose along;
From her lofty latticed window
　　Looked the taylzeour's daughter down,
And she instantly discovered
　　That her heart was not her own.

"Canst thou love me, gentle stranger?"
　　Picking at a pink she stood—
And the knyghte at once admitted
　　That he rather thought he could.
"He who weds me shall have riches,
　　Gold, and lands, and houses free."
"For a single pair of—*small-clothes*,
　　I would roam the world with thee!"

Then she flung him down the tickets
    Well the knyghte their import knew—
"Take this gold, and win thy armour
    From the unbelieving Jew.
Though in garments mean and lowly
    Thou wouldst roam the world with me,
Only as a belted warrior,
    Stranger, will I wed with thee!"

At the feast of good Saint Stitchem,
    In the middle of the spring,
There was some superior jousting,
    By the order of the King.
"Valiant knyghtes!" proclaimed the monarch,
    "You will please to understand,
He who bears himself most bravely
    Shall obtain my daughter's hand."

Well and bravely did they bear them,
    Bravely battled, one and all;
But the bravest in the tourney
    Was a warrior stout and tall.
None could tell his name or lineage,
    None could meet him in the field,
And a goose regardant proper
    Hissed along his azure shield.

"Warrior, thou hast won my daughter!"
    But the champion bowed his knee,
"Royal blood may not be wasted
    On a simple knyghte like me.

She I love is meek and lowly;
　But her heart is kind and free;
Also, there is tin forthcoming,
　Though she is of low degree."

Slowly rose that nameless warrior,
　Slowly turned his steps aside,
Passed the lattice where the princess
　Sate in beauty, sate in pride.
Passed the row of noble ladies,
　Hied him to an humbler seat,
And in silence laid the chaplet
　At the taylzeour's daughter's feet.

The Midnight Visit.

It was the Lord of Castlereagh, he sat within his room,
His arms were crossed upon his breast, his face was marked with gloom;
They said that St Helena's Isle had rendered up its charge,
That France was bristling high in arms—the Emperor at large.

'Twas midnight! all the lamps were dim, and dull
    as death the street,
It might be that the watchman slept that night upon
    his beat,
When lo! a heavy foot was heard to creak upon the
    stair,
The door revolved upon its hinge—Great Heaven!—
    What enters there?

A little man, of stately mien, with slow and solemn
    stride;
His hands are crossed upon his back, his coat is
    opened wide;
And on his vest of green he wears an eagle and a
    star,—
Saint George! protect us! 'tis THE MAN,—the thun-
    der-bolt of war!

Is that the famous hat that waved along Marengo's
    ridge?
Are these the spurs of Austerlitz — the boots of
    Lodi's bridge?

Leads he the conscript swarm again from France's
    hornet hive?
What seeks the fell usurper here, in Britain, and
    alive?

Pale grew the Lord of Castlereagh, his tongue was
    parched and dry,
As in his brain he felt the glare of that tremendous
    eye;
What wonder if he shrank in fear, for who could
    meet the glance
Of him who rear'd, 'mid Russian snows, the gonfalon
    of France?

From the side-pocket of his vest a pinch the despot
    took,
Yet not a whit did he relax the sternness of his look:
"Thou thoughtst the lion was afar, but he hath
    burst the chain—
The watchword for to-night is France—the answer
    St Heléne.

"And didst thou deem the barren isle, or ocean waves, could bind
The master of the universe—the monarch of mankind?
I tell thee, fool! the world itself is all too small for me;
I laugh to scorn thy bolts and bars—I burst them, and am free.

"Thou thinkst that England hates me! Mark!—This very night my name
Was thundered in its capital with tumult and acclaim!
They saw me, knew me, owned my power—Proud lord! I say, beware!
There be men within the Surrey side, who know to do and dare!

"To-morrow in thy very teeth my standard will I rear—
Ay, well that ashen cheek of thine may blanch and shrink with fear!

To-morrow night another town shall sink in ghastly
    flames;
And as I crossed the Borodin, so shall I cross the
    Thames!

"Thou'lt seize me, wilt thou, ere the dawn? Weak
    lordling, do thy worst!
These hands ere now have broke thy chains, thy
    fetters they have burst.
Yet, wouldst thou know my resting-place? Behold,
    'tis written there!
And let thy coward myrmidons approach me if they
    dare!"

Another pinch, another stride—he passes through the
    door—
"Was it a phantom or a man was standing on the
    floor?
And could that be the Emperor that moved before
    my eyes?
Ah, yes! too sure it was himself, for here the paper
    lies!"

With trembling hands Lord Castlereagh undid the mystic scroll,
With glassy eye essayed to read, for fear was on his soul—
"What's here?—'At Astley's, every night, the play of Moscow's Fall!
Napoleon, for the thousandth time, by Mr Gomersal!'"

The Lay of the Lovelorn.

COMRADES, you may pass the rosy. With permission of the chair,
I shall leave you for a little; for I'd like to take the air.

Whether 'twas the sauce at dinner, or that glass of ginger-beer,
Or these strong cheroots, I know not, but I feel a little queer.

Let me go. Nay, Chuckster, blow me, 'pon my
  soul, this is too bad!
When you want me, ask the waiter; he knows where
  I'm to be had.

Whew! This is a great relief now! Let me but
  undo my stock;
Resting here beneath the porch, my nerves will
  steady like a rock.

In my ears I hear the singing of a lot of favourite
  tunes—
Bless my heart, how very odd! Why, surely there's
  a brace of moons!

See! the stars! how bright they twinkle, winking
  with a frosty glare,
Like my faithless cousin Amy when she drove me to
  despair.

Oh, my cousin, spider-hearted! Oh, my Amy! No,
  confound it!
I must wear the mournful willow,—all around my
  heart I've bound it.

Falser than the bank of fancy, frailer than a shilling
    glove,
Puppet to a father's anger, minion to a nabob's love!

Is it well to wish thee happy? Having known me,
    could you ever
Stoop to marry half a heart, and little more than
    half a liver?

Happy! Damme! Thou shalt lower to his level
    day by day,
Changing from the best of china to the commonest
    of clay.

As the husband is, the wife is,—he is stomach-
    plagued and old;
And his curry soups will make thy cheek the colour
    of his gold.

When his feeble love is sated, he will hold thee
    surely then
Something lower than his hookah,—something less
    than his cayenne.

What is this? His eyes are pinky. Was't the
    claret? Oh, no, no,—
Bless your soul! it was the salmon,—salmon always
    makes him so.

Take him to thy dainty chamber—soothe him with
    thy lightest fancies;
He will understand thee, won't he?—pay thee with
    a lover's glances?

Louder than the loudest trumpet, harsh as harshest
    ophicleide,
Nasal respirations answer the endearments of his
    bride.

Sweet response, delightful music! Gaze upon thy
    noble charge,
Till the spirit fill thy bosom that inspired the meek
    Laffarge.

Better thou wert dead before me,—better, better that
    I stood,
Looking on thy murdered body, like the injured
    Daniel Good!

Better thou and I were lying, cold and timber-stiff and dead,
With a pan of burning charcoal underneath our nuptial bed!

Cursed be the Bank of England's notes, that tempt the soul to sin!
Cursed be the want of acres,—doubly cursed the want of tin!

Cursed be the marriage-contract, that enslaved thy soul to greed!
Cursed be the sallow lawyer, that prepared and drew the deed!

Cursed be his foul apprentice, who the loathsome fees did earn!
Cursed be the clerk and parson,—cursed be the whole concern!

※　　＊　　※

Oh, 'tis well that I should bluster,—much I'm like
    to make of that;
Better comfort have I found in singing " All Around
    my Hat."

But that song, so wildly plaintive, palls upon my
    British ears.
'Twill not do to pine for ever,—I am getting up in
    years.

Can't I turn the honest penny, scribbling for the
    weekly press,
And in writing Sunday libels drown my private
    wretchedness?

Oh, to feel the wild pulsation that in manhood's
    dawn I knew,
When my days were all before me, and my years
    were twenty-two!

When I smoked my independent pipe along the
    Quadrant wide,
With the many larks of London flaring up on every
    side;

When I went the pace so wildly, caring little what
    might come;
Coffee-milling care and sorrow, with a nose-adapted
    thumb;

Felt the exquisite enjoyment, tossing nightly off, oh
    heavens!
Brandies at the Cider Cellars, kidneys smoking-hot
    at Evans'!

Or in the Adelphi sitting, half in rapture, half in
    tears,
Saw the glorious melodrama conjure up the shades of
    years!

Saw Jack Sheppard, noble stripling, act his wondrous
    feats again,
Snapping Newgate's bars of iron, like an infant's
    daisy chain.

Might was right, and all the terrors, which had held
    the world in awe,
Were despised, and prigging prospered, spite of
    Laurie, spite of law.

In such scenes as these I triumphed, ere my passion's
    edge was rusted,
And my cousin's cold refusal left me very much disgusted!

Since, my heart is sere and withered, and I do not
    care a curse,
Whether worse shall be the better, or the better be
    the worse.

Hark! my merry comrades call me, bawling for
    another jorum;
They would mock me in derision, should I thus
    appear before 'em.

Womankind no more shall vex me, such at least as
    go arrayed
In the most expensive satins and the newest silk
    brocade.

I'll to Afric, lion-haunted, where the giant forest
    yields
Rarer robes and finer tissue than are sold at Spital
    fields.

Or to burst all chains of habit, flinging habit's self
    aside,
I shall walk the tangled jungle in mankind's primeval
    pride;

Feeding on the luscious berries and the rich cassava
    root,
Lots of dates and lots of guavas, clusters of forbidden
    fruit.

Never comes the trader thither, never o'er the purple
    main
Sounds the oath of British commerce, or the accent
    of Cockaigne.

There, methinks, would be enjoyment, where no
    envious rule prevents;
Sink the steamboats! cuss the railways! rot, O rot
    the Three per Cents!

There the passions, cramped no longer, shall have
    space to breathe, my cousin!
I will wed some savage woman—nay, I'll wed at least
    a dozen.

There I'll rear my young mulattoes, as no Bond Street
    brats are reared:
They shall dive for alligators, catch the wild goats by
    the beard—

Whistle to the cockatoos, and mock the hairy-faced
    baboon,
Worship mighty Mumbo Jumbo in the Mountains of
    the Moon.

I myself, in far Timbuctoo, leopard's blood will daily
    quaff,
Ride a tiger-hunting, mounted on a thorough-bred
    giraffe.

Fiercely shall I shout the war-whoop, as some sullen
    stream he crosses,
Startling from their noonday slumbers iron-bound
    rhinoceroses.

Fool! again the dream, the fancy! But I know my
    words are mad,
For I hold the grey barbarian lower than the Chris-
    tian cad.

I the swell—the city dandy! I to seek such horrid
    places,—
I to haunt with squalid negroes, blubber-lips, and
    monkey-faces!

I to wed with Coromantees! I, who managed—very
    near—
To secure the heart and fortune of the widow Shilli-
    beer!

Stuff and nonsense! let me never fling a single chance
    away;
Maids ere now, I know, have loved me, and another
    maiden may.

'Morning Post' ('The Times' won't trust me) help
    me, as I know you can;
I will pen an advertisement,—that's a never-failing
    plan.

THE LAY OF THE LOVELORN.

"WANTED — By a bard, in wedlock,
    some young interesting woman:
Looks are not so much an object, if the
    shiners be forthcoming!

"Hymen's chains the advertiser vows
    shall be but silken fetters;
Please address to A. T., Chelsea. N.B.
    —You must pay the letters."

That's the sort of thing to do it. Now
    I'll go and taste the balmy,—
Rest thee with thy yellow nabob, spider-
    hearted Cousin Amy!

My Wife's Cousin.

Decked with shoes of blackest polish,
    And with shirt as white as snow,
After early morning breakfast
    To my daily desk I go;
First a fond salute bestowing
    On my Mary's ruby lips,
Which, perchance, may be rewarded
    With a pair of playful nips.

All day long across the ledger
    Still my patient pen I drive,
Thinking what a feast awaits me
    In my happy home at five;

In my small one-storeyed Eden,
    Where my wife awaits my coming,
And our solitary handmaid
    Mutton-chops with care is crumbing.

When the clock proclaims my freedom,
    Then my hat I seize and vanish;
Every trouble from my bosom,
    Every anxious care I banish.
Swiftly brushing o'er the pavement,
    At a furious pace I go,
Till I reach my darling dwelling
    In the wilds of Pimlico.

"Mary, wife, where art thou, dearest?"
    Thus I cry, while yet afar;
Ah! what scent invades my nostrils?—
    'Tis the smoke of a cigar!
Instantly into the parlour
    Like a maniac I haste,
And I find a young Life-Guardsman,
    With his arm round Mary's waist.

MY WIFE'S COUSIN.

And his other hand is playing
    Most familiarly with hers;
And I think my Brussels carpet
    Somewhat damaged by his spurs.
"Fire and furies! what the blazes?"
    Thus in frenzied wrath I call;
When my spouse her arms upraises,
    With a most astounding squall.

"Was there ever such a monster,
    Ever such a wretched wife?
Ah! how long must I endure it,
    How protract this hateful life?
All day long, quite unprotected,
    Does he leave his wife at home;
And she cannot see her cousins,
    Even when they kindly come!"

Then the young Life-Guardsman, rising,
    Scarce vouchsafes a single word,
But, with look of deadly menace,
    Claps his hand upon his sword;

And in fear I faintly falter—
    "This your cousin, then he's mine!
Very glad, indeed, to see you,—
    Won't you stop with us, and dine?"

Won't a ferret suck a rabbit?—
    As a thing of course he stops;
And with most voracious swallow
    Walks into my mutton-chops.
In the twinkling of a bed-post
    Is each savoury platter clear,
And he shows uncommon science
    In his estimate of beer.

Half-and-half goes down before him,
    Gurgling from the pewter pot;
And he moves a counter motion
    For a glass of something hot.
Neither chops nor beer I grudge him,
    Nor a moderate share of goes;
But I know not why he's always
    Treading upon Mary's toes.

MY WIFE'S COUSIN.

Evermore, when, home returning,
    From the counting-house I come,
Do I find the young Life-Guardsman
    Smoking pipes and drinking rum.
Evermore he stays to dinner,
    Evermore devours my meal;
For I have a wholesome horror
    Both of powder and of steel.

Yet I know he's Mary's cousin,
    For my only son and heir
Much resembles that young Guardsman,
    With the self-same curly hair;
But I wish he would not always
    Spoil my carpet with his spurs;
And I'd rather see his fingers
    In the fire, than touching hers.

The Queen in France.

AN ANCIENT SCOTTISH BALLAD.

PART I.

It fell upon the August month,
    When landsmen bide at hame,
That our gude Queen went out to sail
    Upon the saut-sea faem.

And she has ta'en the silk and gowd,
    The like was never seen;
And she has ta'en the Prince Albert,
    And the bauld Lord Aberdeen.

"Ye'se bide at hame, Lord Wellington:
    Ye daurna gang wi' me:
For ye hae been ance in the land o' France,
    And that's eneuch for ye.

"Ye'se bide at hame, Sir Robert Peel,
    To gather the red and the white monie;
And see that my men dinna eat me up
    At Windsor wi' their gluttonie."

They hadna sailed a league, a league,—
    A league, but barely twa,
When the lift grew dark, and the waves grew wan,
    And the wind began to blaw.

"O weel weel may the waters rise,
    In welcome o' their Queen;
What gars ye look sae white, Albert?
    What makes yer ee sae green?"

"My heart is sick, my heid is sair:
    Gie me a glass o' the gude brandie:
To set my foot on the braid green sward,
    I'd gie the half o' my yearly fee.

"It's sweet to hunt the sprightly hare
    On the bonny slopes o' Windsor lea,
But oh, it's ill to bear the thud
    And pitching o' the saut saut sea!"

And aye they sailed, and aye they sailed,
    Till England sank behind,
And over to the coast of France
    They drave before the wind.

Then up and spak the King o' France,
    Was birling at the wine;
"O wha may be the gay ladye,
    That owns that ship sae fine?

"And wha may be that bonny lad,
    That looks sae pale and wan?
I'll wad my lands o' Picardie,
    That he's nae Englishman."

Then up and spak an auld French lord,
    Was sitting beneath his knee,
"It is the Queen o' braid England
    That's come across the sea."

"And oh an it be England's Queen,
    She's welcome here the day;
I'd rather hae her for a friend
    Than for a deadly fae.

"Gae, kill the eerock in the yard,
    The auld sow in the sty,
And bake for her the brockit calf,
    But and the puddock-pie!"

And he has gane until the ship,
    As soon as it drew near,
And he has ta'en her by the hand—
    "Ye're kindly welcome here!"

And syne he kissed her on ae cheek,
    And syne upon the ither;
And he ca'd her his sister dear,
    ' And she ca'd him her brither.

"Light doun, light doun now, ladye mine,
    Light doun upon the shore;
Nae English king has trodden here
    This thousand years and more."

"And gin I lighted on your land,
    As light fu' weel I may,
O am I free to feast wi' you,
    And free to come and gae?"

And he has sworn by the Haly Rood,
    And the black stane o' Dumblane,
That she is free to come and gae
    Till twenty days are gane.

"I've lippened to a Frenchman's aith,"
    Said gude Lord Aberdeen;
"But I'll never lippen to it again,
    Sae lang's the grass is green.

"Yet gae your ways, my sovereign liege,
    Sin' better mayna be;
The wee bit bairns are safe at hame,
    By the blessing o' Marie!"

Then down she lighted frae the ship,
    She lighted safe and sound;
And glad was our good Prince Albert
    To step upon the ground.

"Is that your Queen, my Lord," she said,
    "That auld and buirdly dame?
I see the crown upon her head;
    But I dinna ken her name."

And she has kissed the Frenchman's Queen,
    And eke her daughters three,
And gien her hand to the young Princess,
    That louted upon the knee.

And she has gane to the proud castel,
    That's biggit beside the sea:
But aye, when she thought o' the bairns at hame,
    The tear was in her ee.

She gied the King the Cheshire cheese,
    But and the porter fine;
And he gied her the puddock-pies,
    But and the blude-red wine.

Then up and spak the dourest Prince,
　　An admiral was he;
"Let's keep the Queen o' England here,
　　Sin' better mayna be!

"O mony is the dainty king
　　That we hae trappit here;
And mony is the English yerl
　　That's in our dungeons drear!"

"You lee, you lee, ye graceless loon,
　　Sae loud's I hear ye lee!
There never yet was Englishman
　　That came to skaith by me.

"Gae oot, gae out, ye fause traitour!
　　Gae oot until the street;
It's shame that Kings and Queens should sit
　　Wi' sic a knave at meat!"

Then up and raise the young French lord,
　　In wrath and hie disdain—
"O ye may sit, and ye may eat
　　Your puddock-pies alane!

"But were I in my ain gude ship,
    And sailing wi' the wind,
And did I meet wi' auld Napier,
    I'd tell him o' my mind."

O then the Queen leuch loud and lang,
    And her colour went and came;
"Gin ye meet wi' Charlie on the sea,
    Ye'll wish yersel at hame!"

And aye they birlit at the wine,
    And drank richt merrilie,
Till the auld cock crawed in the castle-yard,
    And the abbey bell struck three.

The Queen she gaed until her bed,
    And Prince Albert likewise;
And the last word that gay ladye said
    Was—"O thae puddock-pies!"

PART II.

The sun was high within the lift
    Afore the French King raise;
And syne he louped intil his sark,
    And warslit on his claes.

"Gae up, gae up, my little foot-page,
    Gae up until the toun;
And gin ye meet wi' the auld harper,
    Be sure ye bring him doun."

And he has met wi' the auld harper;
    O but his een were reid;
And the bizzing o' a swarm o' bees
    Was singing in his heid.

"Alack! alack!" the harper said,
    "That this should e'er hae been!
I daurna gang before my liege,
    For I was fou yestreen."

"It's ye maun come, ye auld harper:
    Ye daurna tarry lang;
The King is just dementit-like
    For wanting o' a sang."

And when he came to the King's chamber,
    He loutit on his knee,
"O what may be your gracious will
    Wi' an auld frail man like me?"

"I want a sang, harper," he said,
    "I want a sang richt speedilie;
And gin ye dinna make a sang,
    I'll hang ye up on the gallows tree."

"I canna do't, my liege," he said,
    "Hae mercy on my auld grey hair!
But gin that I had got the words,
    I think that I might mak the air."

"And wha's to mak the words, fause loon,
    When minstrels we have barely twa;
And Lamartine is in Paris toun,
    And Victor Hugo far awa?"

"The diel may gang for Lamartine,
 And flee away wi' auld Hugo,
For a better minstrel than them baith
 Within this very toun I know.

"O kens my liege the gude Walter,
 At hame they ca' him BON GAULTIER?
He'll rhyme ony day wi' True Thomas,
 And he is in the castle here."

The French King first he lauchit loud,
 And syne did he begin to sing;
"My een are auld, and my heart is cauld,
 Or I suld hae known the minstrels' King.

"Gae take to him this ring o' gowd,
 And this mantle o' the silk sae fine,
And bid him mak a maister sang
 For his sovereign ladye's sake and mine."

"I winna take the gowden ring,
 Nor yet the mantle fine:
But I'll mak the sang for my ladye's sake,
 And for a cup of wine."

K

THE QUEEN IN FRANCE.

The Queen was sitting at the cards,
    The King ahint her back;
And aye she dealed the red honours,
    And aye she dealed the black;

And syne unto the dourest Prince
    She spak richt courteouslie;—
"Now will ye play, Lord Admiral,
    Now will ye play wi' me?"

The dourest Prince he bit his lip,
    And his brow was black as glaur:
"The only game that e'er I play
    Is the bluidy game o' war!"

"And gin ye play at that, young man,
    It weel may cost ye sair;
Ye'd better stick to the game at cards,
    For you'll win nae honours there!"

The King he leuch, and the Queen she leuch,
    Till the tears ran blithely doon;
But the Admiral he raved and swore,
    Till they kicked him frae the room.

The harper came, and the harper sang,
  And oh but they were fain;
For when he had sung the gude sang twice,
  They called for it again.

It was the sang o' the Field o' Gowd,
  In the days of auld langsyne;
When bauld King Henry crossed the seas,
  Wi' his brither King to dine.

And aye he harped, and aye he carped,
  Till up the Queen she sprang—
"I'll wad a County Palatine,
  Gude Walter made that sang."

Three days had come, three days had gane,
  The fourth began to fa',
When our gude Queen to the Frenchman said,
  "It's time I was awa!

"O, bonny are the fields o' France,
  And saftly draps the rain;
But my bairnies are in Windsor Tower,
  And greeting a' their lane.

"Now ye maun come to me, Sir King,
    As I have come to ye;
And a benison upon your heid
    For a' your courtesie!

"Ye maun come, and bring your ladye fere;
    Ye sall na say me no;
And ye'se mind, we have aye a bed to spare
    For that gawsy chield Guizot."

Now he has ta'en her lily-white hand,
    And put it to his lip,
And he has ta'en her to the strand,
    And left her in her ship.

"Will ye come back, sweet bird?" he cried,
    "Will ye come kindly here,
When the lift is blue, and the lavrocks sing,
    In the spring-time o' the year?"

"It's I would blithely come, my Lord,
    To see ye in the spring;
It's I would blithely venture back
    But for ae little thing.

"It isna that the winds are rude,
   Or that the waters rise,
But I loe the roasted beef at hame,
   And no thae puddock-pies!"

The Massacre of the Macpherson.

[FROM THE GAELIC.]

I.

FHAIRSHON swore a feud
 Against the clan M'Tavish;
Marched into their land
 To murder and to rafish;

For he did resolve
    To extirpate the vipers,
With four-and-twenty men
    And five-and-thirty pipers.

II.

But when he had gone
    Half-way down Strath Canaan,
Of his fighting tail
    Just three were remainin'.
They were all he had,
    To back him in ta battle;
All the rest had gone
    Off, to drive ta cattle.

III.

"Fery coot!" cried Fhairshon,
    "So my clan disgraced is;
Lads, we'll need to fight,
    Pefore we touch the peasties.

Here's Mhic-Mac-Methusaleh
    Coming wi' his fassals,
Gillies seventy-three,
    And sixty Dhuinéwassails!"

IV.

"Coot tay to you, sir;
    Are you not ta Fhairshon?
Was you coming here
    To fisit any person?
You are a plackguard, sir!
    It is now six hundred
Coot long years, and more,
    Since my glen was plundered."

V.

"Fat is tat you say?
    Dare you cock your peaver?
I will teach you, sir,
    Fat is coot pehaviour!

You shall not exist
    For another day more;
I will shoot you, sir,
    Or stap you with my claymore!"

VI.

"I am fery glad,
    To learn what you mention,
Since I can prevent
    Any such intention."
So Mhic-Mac-Methusaleh
    Gave some warlike howls,
Trew his skhian-dhu,
    An' stuck it in his powels.

VII.

In this fery way
    Tied ta faliant Fhairshon,
Who was always thought
    A superior person.

Fhairshon had a son,
> Who married Noah's daughter,
And nearly spoiled ta Flood,
> By trinking up ta water:

VIII.

Which he would have done,
> I at least pelieve it,
Had ta mixture peen
> Only half Glenlivet.
This is all my tale:
> Sirs, I hope 'tis new t'ye!
Here's your fery good healths,
> And tamn ta whusky duty!

The Young Stockbroker's Bride.

"O SWIFTLY speed the gallant bark!—
    I say, you mind my luggage, porter!
I do not heed yon storm-cloud dark,
    I go to wed old Jenkin's daughter.
I go to claim my own Mariar,
    The fairest flower that blooms in Harwich;
My panting bosom is on fire,
    And all is ready for the marriage."

Thus spoke young Mivins, as he stepped
    On board the "Firefly," Harwich packet;
The bell rang out, the paddles swept
    Plish-plashing round with noisy racket.
The louring clouds young Mivins saw,
    But fear, he felt, was only folly;
And so he smoked a fresh cigar,
    Then fell to whistling "Nix my dolly!"

The wind it roared; the packet's hulk
    Rocked with a most unpleasant motion;
Young Mivins lent him o'er a bulk,
    And poured his sorrows to the ocean.
Tints—blue and yellow—signs of woe—
    Flushed, rainbow-like, his noble face in,
As suddenly he rushed below,
    Crying, "Steward, steward, bring a basin!"

On sped the bark: the howling storm
    The funnel's tapering smoke did blow far;
Unmoved, young Mivins' lifeless form
    Was stretched upon a haircloth sofar.

All night he moaned, the steamer groaned,
    And he was hourly getting fainter;
When it came bump against the pier,
    And there was fastened by the painter.

Young Mivins rose, arranged his clothes,
    Caught wildly at his small portmanteau;
He was unfit to lie or sit,
    And found it difficult to stand, too.
He sought the deck, he sought the shore,
    He sought the lady's house like winking,
And asked, low tapping at the door,
    "Is this the house of Mr Jenkin?"

A short man came—he told his name—
    Mivins was short—he cut him shorter,
For in a fury he exclaimed,
    "Are you the man as vants my darter?
Vot kim'd on you, last night, young squire?"
    "It was the steamer, rot and scuttle her!"
"Mayhap it vos, but our Mariar
    Valked off last night with Bill the butler.

"And so you've kim'd a post too late."
   "It was the packet, sir, miscarried!"
"Vy, does you think a gal can vait
   As sets 'er 'art on being married?
Last night she vowed she'd be a bride,
   And 'ave a spouse for vuss or better:
So Bill struck in; the knot vos tied,
   And now I vishes you may get her!"

Young Mivins turned him from the spot,
   Bewildered with the dreadful stroke, her
Perfidy came like a shot—
   He was a thunder-struck stockbroker.
"A curse on steam and steamers too!
   By their delays I have been undone!"
He cried, as, looking very blue,
   He rode a bachelor to London.

The Laureates' Tourney.

BY THE HON. T—— B—— M——.

[This and the five following Poems were among those forwarded to the Home Secretary, by the unsuccessful competitors for the Laureateship, on its becoming vacant by the death of Southey. How they came into our possession is a matter between Sir James Graham and ourselves. The result of the contest could never have been doubtful, least of all to the great poet who then succeeded to the bays. His own sonnet on the subject is full of the serene consciousness of superiority, which does not even admit the idea of rivalry, far less of defeat.

    Bays! which in former days have graced the brow
      Of some, who lived and loved, and sang and died;
      Leaves that were gathered on the pleasant side
    Of old Parnassus from Apollo's bough;
    With palpitating hand I take ye now,
      Since worthier minstrel there is none beside,
      And with a thrill of song half deified,
    I bind them proudly on my locks of snow.
    There shall they bide, till he who follows next,
      Of whom I cannot even guess the name,
    Shall by Court favour, or some vain pretext
      Of fancied merit, desecrate the same,—
    And think, perchance, he wears them quite as well
    As the sole bard who sang of Peter Bell!]

FYTTE THE FIRST.

"What news, what news, thou pilgrim grey, what news from southern land?
How fare the bold Conservatives, how is it with Ferrand?

How does the little Prince of Wales—how looks our
    lady Queen?
And tell me, is the monthly nurse once more at
    Windsor seen?"

"I bring no tidings from the Court, nor from St
    Stephen's hall;
I've heard the thundering tramp of horse, and the
    trumpet's battle-call;
And these old eyes have seen a fight, which England
    ne'er hath seen,
Since fell King Richard sobbed his soul through
    blood on Bosworth Green.

'He's dead, he's dead, the Laureate's dead!' 'Twas
    thus the cry began,
And straightway every garret-roof gave up its min-
    strel man;
From Grub Street, and from Houndsditch, and from
    Farringdon Within,
The poets all towards Whitehall poured on with
    eldritch din.

Loud yelled they for Sir James the Graham: but
    sore afraid was he;
A hardy knight were he that might face such a
    minstrelsie.
'Now by St Giles of Netherby, my patron Saint, I
    swear,
I'd rather by a thousand crowns Lord Palmerston
    were here!—

'What is't ye seek, ye rebel knaves—what make you
    there beneath?'
'The bays, the bays! we want the bays! we seek the
    laureate wreath!
We seek the butt of generous wine that cheers the
    sons of song;
Choose thou among us all, Sir Knight—we may not
    tarry long!'

Loud laughed the good Sir James in scorn—'Rare
    jest it were, I think,
But one poor butt of Xeres, and a thousand rogues
    to drink!

An' if it flowed with wine or beer, 'tis easy to be
    seen,
That dry within the hour would be the well of Hip-
    pocrene.

'Tell me, if on Parnassus' heights there grow a
    thousand sheaves:
Or has Apollo's laurel bush yet borne ten hundred
    leaves?
Or if so many leaves were there, how long would
    they sustain
The ravage and the glutton bite of such a locust
    train?

'No! get ye back into your dens, take counsel for
    the night,
And choose me out two champions to meet in deadly
    fight;
To-morrow's dawn shall see the lists marked out in
    Spitalfields,
And he who wins shall have the bays, and he shall
    die who yields!'

Down went the window with a crash,—in silence
    and in fear
Each ragged bard looked anxiously upon his neigh-
    bour near;
Then up and spake young Tennyson—'Who's here
    that fears for death?
'Twere better one of us should die, than England
    lose the wreath!

'Let's cast the lot among us now, which two shall
    fight to-morrow;—
For armour bright we'll club our mite, and horses
    we can borrow;
'Twere shame that bards of France should sneer, and
    German *Dichters* too,
If none of British song might dare a deed of *derring-
    do!*'

'The lists of Love are mine,' said Moore, 'and not
    the lists of Mars;'
Said Hunt, 'I seek the jars of wine, but shun the
    combat's jars!'

'I'm old,' quoth Samuel Rogers. — 'Faith,' says
    Campbell, 'so am I!'
'And I'm in holy orders, sir!' quoth Tom of
    Ingoldsby.

'Now out upon ye, craven loons!' cried Moxon, good
    at need, —
'Bide, if ye will, secure at home, and sleep while
    others bleed.
I second Alfred's motion, boys, — let's try the chance
    of lot;
And monks shall sing, and bells shall ring, for him
    that goes to pot.'

Eight hundred minstrels slunk away — two hundred
    stayed to draw, —
Now Heaven protect the daring wight that pulls the
    longest straw!
'Tis done! 'tis done! And who hath won? Keep
    silence one and all, —
The first is William Wordsworth hight, the second
    Ned Fitzball!

FYTTE THE SECOND.

Oh, bright and gay hath dawned the day on lordly
    Spitalfields,—
How flash the rays with ardent blaze from polished
    helms and shields!
On either side the chivalry of England throng the
    green,
And in the middle balcony appears our gracious
    Queen.

With iron fists, to keep the lists, two valiant knights
    appear,
The Marquis Hal of Waterford, and stout Sir Aubrey
    Vere.
'What ho! there, herald, blow the trump! Let's
    see who comes to claim
The butt of golden Xeres, and the Laureate's
    honoured name!'

That instant dashed into the lists, all armed from
    head to heel,
On courser brown, with vizor down, a warrior
    sheathed in steel;

Then said our Queen—'Was ever seen so stout a
    knight and tall?
His name—his race?'—'An't please your grace, it is
    the brave Fitzball.

'Oft in the Melodrama line his prowess hath been
    shown,
And well throughout the Surrey side his thirst for
    blood is known.
But see, the other champion comes!'—Then rang
    the startled air
With shouts of 'Wordsworth, Wordsworth, ho! the
    bard of Rydal's there.'

And lo! upon a little steed, unmeet for such a
    course,
Appeared the honoured veteran; but weak seemed
    man and horse.
Then shook their ears the sapient peers,—'That joust
    will soon be done:
My Lord of Brougham, I'll back Fitzball, and give
    you two to one!'

'Done,' quoth the Brougham,—'And done with
    you!' 'Now, Minstrels, are you ready?'
Exclaimed the Lord of Waterford,—'You'd better
    both sit steady.
Blow, trumpets, blow the note of charge! and forward
    to the fight!'
'Amen!' said good Sir Aubrey Vere; 'Saint Schism
    defend the right!'

As sweeps the blast against the mast when blows the
    furious squall,
So started at the trumpet's sound the terrible
    Fitzball;
His lance he bore his breast before,—Saint George
    protect the just!
Or Wordsworth's hoary head must roll along the
    shameful dust!

'Who threw that calthrop? Seize the knave!' Alas!
    the deed is done;
Down went the steed, and o'er his head flew bright
    Apollo's son.

'Undo his helmet! cut the lace! pour water on his
    head!'
'It ain't no use at all, my lord; 'cos vy? the covey's
    dead!'

Above him stood the Rydal bard—his face was full
    of woe.
'Now there thou liest, stiff and stark, who never
    feared a foe:
A braver knight, or more renowned in tourney and
    in hall,
Ne'er brought the upper gallery down than terrible
    Fitzball!'

They led our Wordsworth to the Queen—she crowned
    him with the bays,
And wished him many happy years, and many
    quarter-days;
And if you'd have the story told by abler lips than
    mine,
You've but to call at Rydal Mount, and taste the
    Laureate's wine!"

The Royal Banquet.

BY THE HON. G—— S—— S——.

THE Queen she kept high festival in Windsor's lordly hall,
And round her sat the gartered knights, and ermined nobles all;
There drank the valiant Wellington, there fed the wary Peel,
And at the bottom of the board Prince Albert carved the veal.

"What, pantler, ho! remove the cloth! Ho! cellarer, the wine,
And bid the royal nurse bring in the hope of Brunswick's line!"
Then rose with one tumultuous shout the band of British peers,
"God bless her sacred Majesty! Let's see the little dears!"

Now by Saint George, our patron saint, 'twas a touching sight to see
That iron warrior gently place the Princess on his knee;
To hear him hush her infant fears, and teach her how to gape
With rosy mouth expectant for the raisin and the grape!

They passed the wine, the sparkling wine—they filled the goblets up;
Even Brougham, the cynic anchorite, smiled blandly on the cup;

And Lyndhurst, with a noble thirst, that nothing
 could appease,
Proposed the immortal memory of King William on
 his knees.

"What want we here, my gracious liege," cried gay
 Lord Aberdeen,
"Save gladsome song and minstrelsy to flow our
 cups between?
I ask not now for Goulburn's voice or Knatchbull's
 warbling lay,
But where's the Poet Laureate to grace our board to-
 day?"

Loud laughed the Knight of Netherby, and scorn-
 fully he cried,
"Or art thou mad with wine, Lord Earl, or art thy-
 self beside?
Eight hundred Bedlam bards have claimed the
 Laureate's vacant crown,
And now like frantic Bacchanals run wild through
 London town!"

"Now glory to our gracious Queen!" a voice was
    heard to cry,
And dark Macaulay stood before them all with
    frenzied eye;
"Now glory to our gracious Queen, and all her
    glorious race,
A boon, a boon, my sovran liege! Give me the
    Laureate's place!

" 'Twas I that sang the might of Rome, the glories of
    Navarre;
And who could swell the fame so well of Britain's
    Isles afar?
The hero of a hundred fights——" Then Wel-
    lington up sprung,
"Ho, silence in the ranks, I say! Sit down and
    hold your tongue!

"By heaven, thou shalt not twist my name into a
    jingling lay,
Or mimic in thy puny song the thunders of Assaye!

'Tis hard that for thy lust of place in peace we cannot dine.
Nurse, take her Royal Highness, here! Sir Robert, pass the wine!"

"No Laureate need we at our board!" then spoke the Lord of Vaux;
"Here's many a voice to charm the ear with minstrel song, I know.
Even I myself——" Then rose the cry—"A song, a song from Brougham!"
He sang,—and straightway found himself alone within the room.

The Bard of Erin's Lament.

BY T—— M——RE, ESQ.

OH, weep for the hours, when the little blind boy
    Wove round me the spells of his Paphian bower;
When I dipped my light wings in the nectar of joy,
    And soared in the sunshine, the moth of the hour!
From beauty to beauty I passed, like the wind;
    Now fondled the lily, now toyed with the Rose;
And the fair, that at morn had enchanted my mind,
    Was forsook for another ere evening's close.

I sighed not for honour, I cared not for fame,
    While Pleasure sat by me, and Love was my guest;
They twined a fresh wreath for each day as it came,
    And the bosom of Beauty still pillowed my rest:

And the harp of my country—neglected it slept—
    In hall or by greenwood unheard were its songs;
From Love's Sybarite dreams I aroused me, and swept
    Its chords to the tale of her glories and wrongs.

But weep for the hour!—Life's summer is past,
    And the snow of its winter lies cold on my brow;
And my soul, as it shrinks from each stroke of the blast,
    Cannot turn to a fire that glows inwardly now.
No, its ashes are dead—and, alas! Love or Song
    No charm to Life's lengthening shadows can lend,
Like a cup of old wine, rich, mellow, and strong,
    And a seat by the fire *tête-à-tête* with a friend.

The Laureate.

BY A—— T——.

Who would not be
    The Laureate bold,
  With his butt of sherry
  To keep him merry,
And nothing to do but to pocket his gold?

'Tis I would be the Laureate bold!
When the days are hot, and the sun is strong,
I'd lounge in the gateway all the day long,
With her Majesty's footmen in crimson and gold.
I'd care not a pin for the waiting-lord;
But I'd lie on my back on the smooth greensward
With a straw in my mouth, and an open vest,
And the cool wind blowing upon my breast.
And I'd vacantly stare at the clear blue sky,
And watch the clouds that are listless as I,
  Lazily, lazily!
And I'd pick the moss and daisies white,
And chew their stalks with a nibbling bite;
And I'd let my fancies roam abroad
In search of a hint for a birthday ode,
  Crazily, crazily!

Oh, that would be the life for me,
With plenty to get and nothing to do,
But to deck a pet poodle with ribbons of blue,
And whistle all day to the Queen's cockatoo,
  Trance-somely, trance-somely!

M

Then the chambermaids, that clean the rooms,
Would come to the windows and rest on their brooms,
With their saucy caps and their crispèd hair,
And they'd toss their heads in the fragrant air,
And say to each other—"Just look down there,
At the nice young man, so tidy and small,
Who is paid for writing on nothing at all,
    Handsomely, handsomely!"

They would pelt me with matches and sweet pastilles,
And crumpled-up balls of the royal bills,
Giggling and laughing, and screaming with fun,
As they'd see me start, with a leap and a run,
From the broad of my back to the points of my toes,
When a pellet of paper hit my nose,
    Teasingly, sneezingly.
Then I'd fling them bunches of garden flowers,
And hyacinths plucked from the Castle bowers;
And I'd challenge them all to come down to me,
And I'd kiss them all till they kissèd me,
    Laughingly, laughingly.

Oh, would not that be a merry life,
Apart from care and apart from strife,
With the Laureate's wine, and the Laureate's pay,
And no deductions at quarter-day?
Oh, that would be the post for me!
With plenty to get and nothing to do,
But to deck a pet poodle with ribbons of blue,
And whistle a tune to the Queen's cockatoo,
And scribble of verses remarkably few,
And empty at evening a bottle or two,
    Quaffingly, quaffingly!

    'Tis I would be
      The Laureate bold,
    With my butt of sherry
    To keep me merry,
And nothing to do but to pocket my gold!

A Midnight Meditation.

BY SIR E—— B—— L——.

Fill me once more the foaming pewter up!
    Another board of oysters, ladye mine!
To-night Lucullus with himself shall sup.
    These mute inglorious Miltons are divine!
    And as I here in slippered ease recline,
Quaffing of Perkin's Entire my fill,
I sigh not for the lymph of Aganippe's rill.

A nobler inspiration fires my brain,
    Caught from Old England's fine time-hallowed drink;
I snatch the pot again and yet again,
    And as the foaming fluids shrink and shrink,
    Fill me once more, I say, up to the brink!

This makes strong hearts—strong heads attest its
    charm—
This nerves the might that sleeps in Britain's brawny
    arm!

But these remarks are neither here nor there.
    Where was I? Oh, I see—old Southey's dead!
They'll want some bard to fill the vacant chair,
    And drain the annual butt—and oh, what head
    More fit with laurel to be garlanded
Than this, which, curled in many a fragrant coil,
Breathes of Castalia's streams, and best Macassar oil?

I know a grace is seated on my brow,
    Like young Apollo's with his golden beams—
There should Apollo's bays be budding now:—
    And in my flashing eyes the radiance beams,
    That marks the poet in his waking dreams,
When, as his fancies cluster thick and thicker,
He feels the trance divine of poesy and liquor.

They throng around me now, those things of air
    That from my fancy took their being's stamp:

There Pelham sits and twirls his glossy hair,
    There Clifford leads his pals upon the tramp;
    There pale Zanoni, bending o'er his lamp,
Roams through the starry wilderness of thought,
Where all is everything, and everything is nought.

Yes, I am he who sang how Aram won
    The gentle ear of pensive Madeline!
How love and murder hand in hand may run,
    Cemented by philosophy serene,
    And kisses bless the spot where gore has been!
Who breathed the melting sentiment of crime,
And for the assassin waked a sympathy sublime!

Yes, I am he, who on the novel shed
    Obscure philosophy's enchanting light!
Until the public, 'wildered as they read,
    Believed they saw that which was not in sight—
    Of course 'twas not for me to set them right;
For in my nether heart convinced I am,
Philosophy's as good as any other flam.

Novels three-volumed I shall write no more—
　Somehow or other now they will not sell;
And to invent new passions is a bore—
　I find the Magazines pay quite as well.
　Translating's simple, too, as I can tell,
Who've hawked at Schiller on his lyric throne,
And given the astonished bard a meaning all my own.

Moore, Campbell, Wordsworth, their best days are
　　　grassed:
　Battered and broken are their early lyres,
Rogers, a pleasant memory of the past,
　Warmed his young hands at Smithfield's martyr
　　　fires,
　And, worth a plum, nor bays nor butt desires.
But these are things would suit me to the letter,
For though this Stout is good, old Sherry's greatly
　　　better.

A fico for your small poetic ravers,
　Your Hunts, your Tennysons, your Milnes, and
　　　these!
Shall they compete with him who wrote 'Maltravers,'

Prologue to 'Alice or the Mysteries'?
No! Even now my glance prophetic sees
My own high brow girt with the bays about.
What ho! within there, ho! another pint of STOUT!

Stout!   More Stout!!

Montgomery.

A POEM.

Like one who, waking from a troublous dream,
Pursues with force his meditative theme;
Calm as the ocean in its halcyon still,
Calm as the sunlight sleeping on the hill;
Calm as at Ephesus great Paul was seen
To rend his robes in agonies serene;
Calm as the love that radiant Luther bore
To all that lived behind him and before;
Calm as meek Calvin, when, with holy smile,
He sang the mass around Servetus' pile,—
So once again I snatch this harp of mine,
To breathe rich incense from a mystic shrine.
Not now to whisper to the ambient air
The sounds of Satan's Universal Prayer;

Not now to sing, in sweet domestic strife
That woman reigns the Angel of our life;
But to proclaim the wish, with pious art,
Which thrills through Britain's universal heart,—
That on this brow, with native honours graced,
The Laureate's chaplet should at length be placed!

Fear not, ye maids, who love to hear me speak;
Let no desponding tears bedim your cheek!
No gust of envy, no malicious scorn,
Hath this poor heart of mine with frenzy torn.
There are who move so far above the great,
Their very look disarms the glance of hate;
Their thoughts, more rich than emerald or gold,
Enwrap them like the prophet's mantle's fold.
Fear not for me, nor think that this our age,
Blind though it be, hath yet no Archimage.
I, who have bathed, in bright Castalia's tide
By classic Isis and more classic Clyde;
I, who have handled, in my lofty strain,
All things divine, and many things profane;
I, who have trod where seraphs fear to tread;
I, who on mount——no, "honey-dew" have fed;

I, who undaunted broke the mystic seal,
And left no page for prophets to reveal;
I, who in shade portentous Dante threw;
I, who have done what Milton dared not do,—
I fear no rival for the vacant throne;
No mortal thunder shall eclipse my own!

Let dark Macaulay chant his Roman lays,
Let Monckton Milnes go maunder for the bays,
Let Simmons call on great Napoleon's shade,
Let Lytton Bulwer seek his Aram's aid,
Let Wordsworth ask for help from Peter Bell,
Let Campbell carol Copenhagen's knell,
Let Delta warble through his Delphic groves,
Let Elliott shout for pork and penny loaves,—
I care not, I! resolved to stand or fall;
One down, another on, I'll smash them all!

Back, ye profane! this hand alone hath power
To pluck the laurel from its sacred bower;
This brow alone is privileged to wear
The ancient wreath o'er hyacinthine hair;
These lips alone may quaff the sparkling wine,

And make its mortal juice once more divine.
Back, ye profane! And thou, fair Queen, rejoice:
A nation's praise shall consecrate thy choice.
Thus, then, I kneel where Spenser knelt before,
On the same spot, perchance, of Windsor's floor;
And take, while awe-struck millions round me stand,
The hallowed wreath from great Victoria's hand.

The Death of Space.

[Why has Satan's own Laureate never given to the world his marvellous threnody on the "Death of Space"? Who knows where the bays might have fallen, had he forwarded that mystic manuscript to the Home Office? If unwonted modesty withholds it from the public eye, the public will pardon the boldness that tears from blushing obscurity the following fragments of this unique poem.]

ETERNITY shall raise her funeral-pile
   In the vast dungeon of the extinguished sky,
And, clothed in dim barbaric splendour, smile,
   And murmur shouts of elegiac joy.

While those that dwell beyond the realms of space,
   And those that people all that dreary void,
When old Time's endless heir hath run his race,
   Shall live for aye, enjoying and enjoyed.

And 'mid the agony of unsullied bliss,
   Her Demogorgon's doom shall Sin bewail,
The undying serpent at the spheres shall hiss,
   And lash the empyrean with his tail.

And Hell, inflated with supernal wrath,
    Shall open wide her thunder-bolted jaws,
And shout into the dull cold ear of Death,
    That he must pay his debt to Nature's laws.

And when the King of Terrors breathes his last,
    Infinity shall creep into her shell,
Cause and effect shall from their thrones be cast,
    And end their strife with suicidal yell:

While from their ashes, burnt with pomp of kings,
    'Mid incense floating to the evanished skies,
Nonenity, on circumambient wings,
    An everlasting Phœnix shall arise.

Little John and the Red Friar.

A LAY OF SHERWOOD.

FYTTE THE FIRST.

The deer may leap within the glade;
    The fawns may follow free—
For Robin is dead, and his bones are laid
    Beneath the greenwood tree.

And broken are his merry, merry men,
　That goodly companie:
There's some have ta'en the northern road
　With Jem of Netherbee.

The best and bravest of the band
　With Derby Ned are gone;
But Earlie Grey and Charlie Wood,
　They stayed with Little John.

Now Little John was an outlaw proud,
　A prouder ye never saw;
Through Nottingham and Leicester shires
　He thought his word was law,
And he strutted through the greenwood wide,
　Like a pestilent jackdaw.

He swore that none, but with leave of him,
　Should set foot on the turf so free:
And he thought to spread his cutter's rule,
　All over the south countrie.
"There's never a knave in the land," he said,
　"But shall pay his toll to me!"

And Charlie Wood was a taxman good
    As ever stepped the ground,
He levied mail, like a sturdy thief,
    From all the yeomen round.
"Nay, stand!" quoth he, "thou shalt pay to me
    Seven pence from every pound!"

Now word has come to Little John,
    As he lay upon the grass,
That a Friar red was in merry Sherwood
    Without his leave to pass.

"Come hither, come hither, my little foot-page!
    Ben Hawes, come tell to me,
What manner of man is this burly frere
    Who walks the wood so free?"

"My master good!" the little page said,
    "His name I wot not well,
But he wears on his head a hat so red,
    With a monstrous scallop-shell.

"He says he is Prior of Copmanshurst,
    And Bishop of London town,
And he comes with a rope from our father the Pope,
    To put the outlaws down.

"I saw him ride but yester-tide,
    With his jolly chaplains three;
And he swears that he has an open pass
    From Jem of Netherbee!"

Little John has ta'en an arrow so broad,
    And broken it o'er his knee;
"Now may I never strike doe again,
    But this wrong avenged shall be!

"And has he dared, this greasy frere,
    To trespass in my bound,
Nor asked for leave from Little John
    To range with hawk and hound?

"And has he dared to take a pass
    From Jem of Netherbee,
Forgetting that the Sherwood shaws
    Pertain of right to me?

"O were he but a simple man,
    And not a slip-shod frere!
I'd hang him up by his own waist-rope
    Above yon tangled brere.

"O did he come alone from Jem,
    And not from our father the Pope,
I'd bring him into Copmanshurst,
    With the noose of a hempen rope!

" But since he has come from our father the Pope,
    And sailed across the sea,
And since he has power to bind and lose,
    His life is safe for me;
But a heavy penance he shall do
    Beneath the greenwood tree!"

"O tarry yet!" quoth Charlie Wood,
    "O tarry, master mine!
It's ill to shear a yearling hog,
    Or twist the wool of swine!

"It's ill to make a bonny silk purse
    From the ear of a bristly boar;
It's ill to provoke a shaveling's curse,
    When the way lies him before.

"I've walked the forest for twenty years,
    In wet weather and dry,
And never stopped a good fellowe,
    Who had no coin to buy.

"What boots it to search a beggarman's bags,
    When no silver groat he has?
So, master mine, I rede you well,
    E'en let the friar pass!"

"Now cease thy prate," quoth Little John,
    "Thou japest but in vain;
An he have not a groat within his pouch,
    We may find a silver chain.

"But were he as bare as a new-flayed buck,
    As truly he may be,
He shall not tread the Sherwood shaws
    Without the leave of me!"

Little John has taken his arrows and bow,
  His sword and buckler strong,
And lifted up his quarter-staff,
  Was full three cloth yards long.

And he has left his merry men
  At the trysting-tree behind,
And gone into the gay greenwood,
  This burly frere to find.

O'er holt and hill, through brake and brere,
  He took his way alone—
Now, Lordlings, list and you shall hear
  This geste of Little John.

FYTTE THE SECOND.

'Tis merry, 'tis merry in gay greenwood,
  When the little birds are singing,
When the buck is belling in the fern,
  And the hare from the thicket springing!

'Tis merry to hear the waters clear,
    As they splash in the pebbly fall;
And the ouzel whistling to his mate,
    As he lights on the stones so small.

But small pleasaunce took Little John
    In all he heard and saw;
Till he reached the cave of a hermit old
    Who wonned within the shaw.

" *Ora pro nobis!* " quoth Little John—
    His Latin was somewhat rude—
" Now, holy father, hast thou seen
    A frere within the wood?

" By his scarlet hose, and his ruddy nose,
    I guess you may know him well;
And he wears on his head a hat so red,
    And a monstrous scallop-shell."

" I have served Saint Pancras," the hermit said,
    " In this cell for thirty year,
Yet never saw I, in the forest bounds,
    The face of such a frere!

"An' if ye find him, master mine,
    E'en take an old man's advice,
An' raddle him well, till he roar again,
    Lest ye fail to meet him twice!"

"Trust me for that!" quoth Little John—
    "Trust me for that!" quoth he, with a laugh;
"There never was man of woman born,
    That asked twice for the taste of my quarter-staff!"

Then Little John, he strutted on,
    Till he came to an open bound,
And he was aware of a Red Friar,
    Was sitting upon the ground.

His shoulders they were broad and strong,
    And large was he of limb;
Few yeomen in the north countrie
    Would care to mell with him.

He heard the rustling of the boughs,
    As Little John drew near;
But never a single word he spoke,
    Of welcome or of cheer:

Less stir he made than a pedlar would
    For a small gnat in his ear!

I like not his looks! thought Little John,
    Nor his staff of the oaken tree.
Now may our Lady be my help,
    Else beaten I well may be!

"What dost thou here, thou strong Friar,
    In Sherwood's merry round,
Without the leave of Little John,
    To range with hawk and hound?"

"Small thought have I," quoth the Red Friar,
    "Of any leave, I trow;
That Little John is an outlawed thief,
    And so, I ween, art thou!

"Know, I am Prior of Copmanshurst,
    And Bishop of London town,
And I bring a rope from our father the Pope,
    To put the outlaws down."

Then out spoke Little John in wrath,
  "I tell thee, burly frere,
The Pope may do as he likes at home,
  But he sends no Bishops here!

"Up, and away, Red Friar!" he said,
  "Up, and away, right speedilie;
An it were not for that cowl of thine,
  Avenged on thy body I would be!"

"Nay, heed not that," said the Red Friar,
  "And let my cowl no hindrance be;
I warrant that I can give as good
  As ever I think to take from thee!"

Little John he raised his quarter-staff,
  And so did the burly priest,
And they fought beneath the greenwood tree
  A stricken hour at least.

But Little John was weak of fence,
  And his strength began to fail;
Whilst the Friar's blows came thundering down,
  Like the strokes of a threshing-flail.

"Now hold thy hand, thou stalwart Friar,
 Now rest beneath the thorn,
Until I gather breath enow,
 For a blast at my bugle-horn!"

"I'll hold my hand," the Friar said,
 "Since that is your propine,
But, an you sound your bugle-horn,
 I'll even blow on mine!"

Little John he wound a blast so shrill,
 That it rang o'er rock and linn,
And Charlie Wood, and his merry men all,
 Came lightly bounding in.

The Friar he wound a blast so strong
 That it shook both bush and tree,
And to his side came witless Will,
 And Jem of Netherbee;
With all the worst of Robin's band,
 And many a Rapparee!

LITTLE JOHN AND THE RED FRIAR.

Little John he wist not what to do,
    When he saw the others come;
So he twisted his quarter-staff between
    His fingers and his thumb.

"There's some mistake, good Friar!" he said,
    "There's some mistake 'twixt thee and me;
I know thou art Prior of Copmanshurst,
    But not beneath the greenwood tree.

"And if you will take some other name,
    You shall have ample leave to bide;
With pasture also for your Bulls,
    And power to range the forest wide."

"There's no mistake!" the Friar said;
    "I'll call myself just what I please.
My doctrine is that chalk is chalk,
    And cheese is nothing else than cheese."

"So be it, then!" quoth Little John;
    "But surely you will not object,
If I and all my merry men
    Should treat you with reserved respect?

"We can't call you Prior of Copmanshurst,
 Nor Bishop of London town,
Nor on the grass, as you chance to pass,
 Can we very well kneel down.

"But you'll send the Pope my compliments,
  And say, as a further hint,
That, within the Sherwood bounds, you saw
Little John, who is the son-in-law
  Of his friend, old Mat-o'-the-Mint!"

So ends this geste of Little John—
  God save our noble Queen!
But, Lordlings, say—Is Sherwood now
  What Sherwood once hath been?

The Rhyme of Sir Launcelot Bogle.

A LEGEND OF GLASGOW.

BY MRS E—— B—— B——.

There's a pleasant place of rest, near a City of the West,
Where its bravest and its best find their grave.

Below the willows weep, and their hoary branches
    sleep
  In the waters still and deep,
            Not a wave!

And the old Cathedral Wall, so scathed and grey
    and tall,
  Like a priest surveying all, stands beyond;
And the ringing of its bell, when the ringers ring it
    well,
  Makes a kind of tidal swell
            On the pond!

And there it was I lay, on a beauteous summer's day,
  With the odour of the hay floating by;
And I heard the blackbirds sing, and the bells de-
    murely ring,
  Chime by chime, ting by ting,
            Droppingly.

Then my thoughts went wandering back, on a very
    beaten track,
  To the confine deep and black of the tomb;

And I wondered who he was, that is laid beneath
    the grass,
  Where the dandelion has
        Such a bloom.

Then I straightway did espy, with my slantly-sloping
    eye,
  A carvèd stone hard by, somewhat worn;
And I read in letters cold—𝔥𝔢𝔯𝔢 . 𝔩𝔶𝔢𝔰 . 𝔏𝔞𝔲𝔫𝔠𝔢𝔩𝔬𝔱 .
    𝔶𝔢 . 𝔟𝔬𝔩𝔡𝔢,
  𝔒𝔣𝔣 . 𝔶𝔢 . 𝔯𝔞𝔠𝔢 . 𝔬𝔣𝔣 . 𝔅𝔬𝔤𝔦𝔩𝔢 . 𝔬𝔩𝔡,
      𝔊𝔩𝔞𝔰𝔤𝔬𝔴 . 𝔟𝔬𝔯𝔫𝔢.

𝔥𝔢 . 𝔴𝔞𝔩𝔰 . 𝔞𝔫𝔢 . 𝔟𝔞𝔩𝔤𝔞𝔲𝔫𝔱 . 𝔨𝔫𝔶𝔤𝔥𝔱𝔢 . 𝔪𝔞𝔦𝔰𝔱 . 𝔱𝔢𝔯𝔯𝔦𝔟𝔩𝔢 . 𝔦𝔫 .
    𝔣𝔶𝔠𝔥𝔱𝔢.
Here the letters failed outright, but I knew
That a stout crusading lord, who had crossed the
    Jordan's ford,
  Lay there beneath the sward,
        Wet with dew.

Time and tide they passed away, on that pleasant
    summer's day,
  And around me, as I lay, all grew old:

Sank the chimneys from the town, and the clouds of
vapour brown
No longer, like a crown,
O'er it rolled.

Sank the great Saint Rollox stalk, like a pile of
dingy chalk;
Disappeared the cypress walk, and the flowers;
And a donjon-keep arose, that might baffle any foes,
With its men-at-arms in rows,
On the towers.

And the flag that flaunted there showed the grim
and grizzly bear,
Which the Bogles always wear for their crest.
And I heard the warder call, as he stood upon the
wall,
"Wake ye up! my comrades all,
From your rest!

"For, by the blessed rood, there's a glimpse of armour
good
In the deep Cowcaddens wood, o'er the stream;

And I hear the stifled hum of a multitude that come,
  Though they have not beat the drum,
            It would seem!

"Go tell it to my Lord, lest he wish to man the ford
  With partisan and sword, just beneath;
Ho, Gilkison and Nares! Ho, Provan of Cowlairs!
  We'll back the bonny bears
            To the death!"

To the tower above the moat, like one who heedeth not,
  Came the bold Sir Launcelot, half undressed;
On the outer rim he stood, and peered into the wood,
  With his arms across him glued
            On his breast.

And he muttered, "Foe accurst! hast thou dared to
  seek me first?
  George of Gorbals, do thy worst—for I swear,
O'er thy gory corpse to ride, ere thy sister and my
  bride,
  From my undissevered side
            Thou shalt tear!

THE RHYME OF SIR LAUNCELOT BOGLE.

"Ho, herald mine, Brownlee! ride forth, I pray, and
see,
Who, what, and whence is he, foe or friend!
Sir Roderick Dalgleish, and my foster-brother Neish,
With his bloodhounds in the leash,
Shall attend."

Forth went the herald stout, o'er the drawbridge and
without,
Then a wild and savage shout rose amain,
Six arrows sped their force, and, a pale and bleeding
corse,
He sank from off his horse
On the plain!

Back drew the bold Dalgleish, back started stalwart
Neish,
With his bloodhounds in the leash, from Brownlee.
"Now shame be to the sword that made thee knight
and lord,
Thou caitiff thrice abhorred,
Shame on thee!

"Ho, bowmen, bend your bows! Discharge upon
 the foes
　Forthwith no end of those heavy bolts.
Three angels to the brave who finds the foe a grave,
　And a gallows for the slave
　　　　　　Who revolts!"

Ten days the combat lasted; but the bold defenders
　fasted,
　While the foemen, better pastied, fed their host;
You might hear the savage cheers of the hungry
　Gorbaliers,
　As at night they dressed the steers
　　　　　　For the roast.

And Sir Launcelot grew thin, and Provan's double
　chin
　Showed sundry folds of skin down beneath;
In silence and in grief found Gilkison relief,
　Nor did Neish the spell-word, beef,
　　　　　　Dare to breathe.

To the ramparts Edith came, that fair and youthful
    dame,
  With the rosy evening flame on her face.
She sighed, and looked around on the soldiers on
    the ground,
  Who but little penance found,
            Saying grace!

And she said unto her lord, as he leaned upon his
    sword,
  "One short and little word may I speak?
I cannot bear to view those eyes so ghastly blue,
  Or mark the sallow hue
            Of thy cheek!

"I know the rage and wrath that my furious brother
    hath
  Is less against us both than at me.
Then, dearest, let me go, to find among the foe
  An arrow from the bow,
            Like Brownlee!"

"I would soil my father's name, I would lose my
    treasured fame,
  Ladye mine, should such a shame on me light:
While I wear a belted brand, together still we stand,
  Heart to heart, hand in hand!"
                Said the knight.

"All our chances are not lost, as your brother and
    his host
  Shall discover to their cost rather hard!
Ho, Provan! take this key—hoist up the Malvoisie,
  And heap it, d'ye see,
                In the yard.

"Of usquebaugh and rum, you will find, I reckon,
    some,
  Besides the beer and mum, extra stout;
Go straightway to your tasks, and roll me all the
    casks,
  As also range the flasks,
                Just without.

"If I know the Gorbaliers, they are sure to dip their
    ears
  In the very inmost tiers of the drink.
Let them win the outer court, and hold it for their
    sport,
  Since their time is rather short,
              I should think!"

With a loud triumphant yell, as the heavy draw-
    bridge fell,
  Rushed the Gorbaliers pell-mell, wild as Druids;
Mad with thirst for human gore, how they threatened
    and they swore,
  Till they stumbled on the floor,
              O'er the fluids.

Down their weapons then they threw, and each
    savage soldier drew
  From his belt an iron screw, in his fist;
George of Gorbals found it vain their excitement to
    restrain,
  And indeed was rather fain
              To assist.

With a beaker in his hand, in the midst he took his
 stand,
 And silence did command, all below—
"Ho! Launcelot the bold, ere thy lips are icy cold,
 In the centre of thy hold,
 Pledge me now!

"Art surly, brother mine? In this cup of rosy wine,
 I drink to the decline of thy race!
Thy proud career is done, thy sand is nearly run,
 Never more shall setting sun
 Gild thy face!

"The pilgrim, in amaze, shall see a goodly blaze,
 Ere the pallid morning rays flicker up;
And perchance he may espy certain corpses swinging
 high!
 What, brother! art thou dry?
 Fill my cup!"

Dumb as death stood Launcelot, as though he heard
 him not,
 But his bosom Provan smote, and he swore:

And Sir Roderick Dalgleish remarked aside to Neish,
  "Never sure did thirsty fish
            Swallow more!

"Thirty casks are nearly done, yet the revel's scarce
     begun;
  It were knightly sport and fun to strike in!"
"Nay, tarry till they come," quoth Neish, "unto the
     rum—
  They are working at the mum,
            And the gin!"

Then straight there did appear to each gallant
     Gorbalier
  Twenty castles dancing near, all around;
The solid earth did shake, and the stones beneath
     them quake,
  And sinuous as a snake
            Moved the ground.

Why and wherefore they had come, seemed intricate
     to some,
  But all agreed the rum was divine.

And they looked with bitter scorn on their leader highly born,
  Who preferred to fill his horn
      Up with wine!

Then said Launcelot the tall, "Bring the chargers from their stall;
  Lead them straight unto the hall, down below:
Draw your weapons from your side, fling the gates asunder wide,
  And together we shall ride
      On the foe!"

Then Provan knew full well, as he leaped into his selle,
  That few would 'scape to tell how they fared;
And Gilkison and Nares, both mounted on their mares,
  Looked terrible as bears,
      All prepared.

With his bloodhounds in the leash, stood the iron-sinewed Neish,
  And the falchion of Dalgleish glittered bright—

"Now, wake the trumpet's blast; and, comrades, follow fast;
  Smite them down unto the last!"
                    Cried the knight.

In the cumbered yard without, there was shriek, and yell, and shout,
  As the warriors wheeled about, all in mail.
On the miserable kerne fell the death-strokes stiff and stern,
  As the deer treads down the fern,
                    In the vale!

Saint Mungo be my guide! It was goodly in that tide
  To see the Bogle ride in his haste;
He accompanied each blow with a cry of "Ha!" or "Ho!"
  And always cleft the foe
                    To the waist.

"George of Gorbals—craven lord! thou didst threat me with the cord;
  Come forth and brave my sword, if you dare!"

But he met with no reply, and never could descry
    The glitter of his eye
            Anywhere.

Ere the dawn of morning shone, all the Gorbaliers
    were down,
    Like a field of barley mown in the ear:
It had done a soldier good to see how Provan stood,
    With Neish all bathed in blood,
           Panting near.

"Now bend ye to your tasks—go carry down those
    casks,
    And place the empty flasks on the floor;
George of Gorbals scarce will come, with trumpet and
    with drum,
    To taste our beer and rum
           Any more!"

So they bent them to their tasks, and they carried
    down the casks,
    And replaced the empty flasks on the floor;

But pallid for a week was the cellar-master's cheek,
    For he swore he heard a shriek
              Through the door.

When the merry Christmas came, and the Yule-log
    lent its flame
To the face of squire and dame in the hall,
The cellarer went down to tap October brown,
    Which was rather of renown
              'Mongst them all.

He placed the spigot low, and gave the cask a blow,
    But his liquor would not flow through the pin.
"Sure, 'tis sweet as honeysuckles!" so he rapped it
    with his knuckles,
  But a sound, as if of buckles,
              Clashed within.

"Bring a hatchet, varlets, here!" and they cleft the
    cask of beer:
  What a spectacle of fear met their sight!

There George of Gorbals lay, skull and bones all
    blanched and grey,
  In the arms he bore the day
        Of the fight!

I have sung this ancient tale, not, I trust, without
    avail,
  Though the moral ye may fail to perceive;
Sir Launcelot is dust, and his gallant sword is rust,
  And now, I think, I must
        Take my leave!

The Lay of the Lover's Friend.

[AIR—"*The days we went a-gypsying.*"]

I WOULD all womankind were dead,
    Or banished o'er the sea;
For they have been a bitter plague
    These last six weeks to me:
It is not that I'm touched myself,
    For that I do not fear;

No female face has shown me grace
  For many a bygone year.
    But 'tis the most infernal bore,
      Of all the bores I know,
     To have a friend who's lost his heart
      A short time ago.

Whene'er we steam it to Blackwall,
  Or down to Greenwich run,
To quaff the pleasant cider-cup,
  And feed on fish and fun;
Or climb the slopes of Richmond Hill,
  To catch a breath of air:
Then, for my sins, he straight begins
  To rave about his fair.
    Oh, 'tis the most tremendous bore,
      Of all the bores I know,
     To have a friend who's lost his heart
      A short time ago.

In vain you pour into his ear
  Your own confiding grief;

In vain you claim his sympathy,
    In vain you ask relief;
In vain you try to rouse him by
    Joke, repartee, or quiz;
His sole reply's a burning sigh,
    And "What a mind it is!"
        O Lord! it is the greatest bore,
            Of all the bores I know,
        To have a friend who's lost his heart
            A short time ago.

I've heard her thoroughly described
    A hundred times, I'm sure;
And all the while I've tried to smile,
    And patiently endure;
He waxes strong upon his pangs,
    And potters o'er his grog;
And still I say, in a playful way—
    "Why, you're a lucky dog!"
        But oh! it is the heaviest bore,
            Of all the bores I know,
        To have a friend who's lost his heart
            A short time ago.

I really wish he'd do like me,
    When I was young and strong;
I formed a passion every week,
    But never kept it long.
But he has not the sportive mood
    That always rescued me,
And so I would all women could
    Be banished o'er the sea.
      For 'tis the most egregious bore,
        Of all the bores I know,
      To have a friend who's lost his heart
      A short time ago.

Francesca Da Rimini.

TO BON GAULTIER.

[ARGUMENT.—An impassioned pupil of Leigh Hunt, having met Bon Gaultier at a Fancy Ball, declares the destructive consequences thus.]

Didst thou not praise me, Gaultier, at the ball,
Ripe lips, trim boddice, and a waist so small,
With clipsome lightness, dwindling ever less,
Beneath the robe of pea-y greeniness?
Dost thou remember, when, with stately prance,
Our heads went crosswise in the country-dance;
How soft, warm fingers, tipped like buds of balm,
Trembled within the squeezing of thy palm;

And how a cheek grew flushed and peachy-wise
At the frank lifting of thy cordial eyes?
Ah, me! that night there was one gentle thing,
Who, like a dove, with its scarce feathered wing,
Fluttered at the approach of thy quaint swaggering!

There's wont to be, at conscious times like these,
An affectation of a bright-eyed ease,—
A crispy cheekiness, if so I dare
Describe the swaling of a jaunty air;
And thus, when swirling from the waltz's wheel,
You craved my hand to grace the next quadrille,
That smiling voice, although it made me start,
Boiled in the meek o'erlifting of my heart;
And, picking at my flowers, I said, with free
And usual tone, "O yes, sir, certainly!"

Like one that swoons, 'twixt sweet amaze and fear,
I heard the music burning in my ear,
And felt I cared not, so thou wert with me,
If Gurth or Wamba were our vis-à-vis.
So, when a tall Knight Templar ringing came,
And took his place amongst us with his dame,
I neither turned away, nor bashful shrunk
From the stern survey of the soldier-monk,

Though rather more than three full quarters drunk;
But, threading through the figure, first in rule,
I paused to see thee plunge into La Poule.

Ah, what a sight was that! Not prurient Mars,
Pointing his toe through ten celestial bars—
Not young Apollo, beamily arrayed
In tripsome guise for Juno's masquerade—
Not smartest Hermes, with his pinion girth,
Jerking with freaks and snatches down to earth,
Looked half so bold, so beautiful, and strong,
As thou, when pranking through the glittering throng!
How the calmed ladies looked with eyes of love
On thy trim velvet doublet laced above;
The hem of gold, that, like a wavy river,
Flowed down into thy back with glancing shiver!
So bare was thy fine throat, and curls of black,
So lightsomely dropped in thy lordly back,
So crisply swaled the feather in thy bonnet,
So glanced thy thigh, and spanning palm upon it,
That my weak soul took instant flight to thee,
Lost in the fondest gush of that sweet witchery!

But when the dance was o'er, and arm in arm
(The full heart beating 'gainst the elbow warm)

We passed into the great refreshment-hall,
Where the heaped cheese-cakes and the comfits small
Lay, like a hive of sunbeams, brought to burn
Around the margin of the negus urn;
When my poor quivering hand you fingered twice,
And, with inquiring accents, whispered " Ice,
Water, or cream ?" I could no more dissemble,
But dropped upon the couch all in a tremble.
A swimming faintness misted o'er my brain,
The corks seemed starting from the brisk champagne,
The custards fell untouched upon the floor,
Thine eyes met mine. That night we danced no more !

The Cadi's Daughter.

A LEGEND OF THE BOSPHORUS.

[FROM ANY OF THE ANNUALS.]

How beauteous is the star of night
    Within the eastern skies,
Like the twinkling glance of the Toorkman's lance,
    Or the antelope's azure eyes!

A lamp of love in the heaven above,
    That star is fondly streaming;
And the gay kiosk and the shadowy mosque
    In the Golden Horn are gleaming.

Young Leila sits in her jasmine bower,
    And she hears the bulbul sing,
As it thrills its throat to the first full note,
    That anthems the flowery spring.
She gazes still, as a maiden will,
    On that beauteous eastern star:
You might see the throb of her bosom's sob
    Beneath the white cymar!

She thinks of him who is far away,—
    Her own brave Galiongee,—
Where the billows foam and the breezes roam,
    On the wild Carpathian sea.
She thinks of the oath that bound them both
    Beside the stormy water;
And the words of love, that in Athens' grove
    He spake to the Cadi's daughter.

"My Selim!" thus the maiden said,
　"Though severed thus we be
By the raging deep and the mountain steep,
　My soul still yearns to thee.
Thy form so dear is mirrored here
　In my heart's pellucid well,
As the rose looks up to Phingari's orb,
　Or the moth to the gay gazelle.

"I think of the time when the Kaftan's crime
　Our love's young joys o'ertook,
And thy name still floats in the plaintive notes
　Of my silver-toned chibouque.
Thy hand is red with the blood it has shed,
　Thy soul it is heavy laden;
Yet come, my Giaour, to thy Leila's bower;
　Oh, come to thy Turkish maiden!"

A light step trod on the dewy sod,
　And a voice was in her ear,
And an arm embraced young Leila's waist—
　"Belovèd! I am here!"

Like the phantom form that rules the storm,
    Appeared the pirate lover,
And his fiery eye was like Zatanai,
    As he fondly bent above her.

"Speak, Leila, speak; for my light caïque
    Rides proudly in yonder bay;
I have come from my rest to her I love best,
    To carry thee, love, away.
The breast of thy lover shall shield thee, and cover
    My own jemscheed from harm;
Think'st thou I fear the dark vizier,
    Or the mufti's vengeful arm?

"Then droop not, love, nor turn away
    From this rude hand of mine!"
And Leila looked in her lover's eyes,
    And murmured—"I am thine!"
But a gloomy man with a yataghan
    Stole through the acacia-blossoms,
And the thrust he made with his gleaming blade
    Hath pierced through both their bosoms.

"There! there! thou cursèd caitiff Giaour!
  There, there, thou false one, lie!"
Remorseless Hassan stands above,
  And he smiles to see them die.
They sleep beneath the fresh green turf,
  The lover and the lady—
And the maidens wail to hear the tale
  Of the daughter of the Cadi!

The Dirge of the Drinker.

Brothers, spare awhile your liquor, lay your final
    tumbler down;
He has dropped—that star of honour—on the field
    of his renown!
Raise the wail, but raise it softly, lowly bending on
    your knees,
If you find it more convenient, you may hiccup if
    you please.
Sons of Pantagruel, gently let your hip-hurrahing sink,
Be your manly accents clouded, half with sorrow,
    half with drink!
Lightly to the sofa pillow lift his head from off the
    floor;
See, how calm he sleeps, unconscious as the deadest
    nail in door!
Widely o'er the earth I've wandered; where the
    drink most freely flowed,
I have ever reeled the foremost, foremost to the
    beaker strode.

Deep in shady Cider Cellars I have dreamed o'er
    heavy wet,
By the fountains of Damascus I have quaffed the
    rich sherbet,
Regal Montepulciano drained beneath its native rock,
On Johannis' sunny mountain frequent hiccuped o'er
    my hock;
I have bathed in butts of Xeres deeper than did e'er
    Monsoon,
Sangaree'd with bearded Tartars in the Mountains
    of the Moon;
In beer-swilling Copenhagen I have drunk your
    Danesman blind,
I have kept my feet in Jena, when each bursch to
    earth declined;
Glass for glass, in fierce Jamaica, I have shared the
    planter's rum.
Drunk with Highland dhuiné-wassails, till each gib-
    bering Gael grew dumb;
But a stouter, bolder drinker—one that loved his
    liquor more—
Never yet did I encounter than our friend upon the
    floor!

Yet the best of us are mortal, we to weakness all are heir,
He has fallen who rarely staggered—let the rest of us beware!
We shall leave him as we found him,—lying where his manhood fell,
'Mong the trophies of the revel, for he took his tipple well.
Better 'twere we loosed his neckcloth, laid his throat and bosom bare,
Pulled his Hobies off, and turned his toes to taste the breezy air.
Throw the sofa-cover o'er him, dim the flaring of the gas,
Calmly, calmly let him slumber, and, as by the bar we pass,
We shall bid that thoughtful waiter place beside him, near and handy,
Large supplies of soda-water, tumblers bottomed well with brandy,
So, when waking, he shall drain them, with that deathless thirst of his,—
Clinging to the hand that smote him, like a good 'un as he is!

The Death of Duval.

BY W—— H—— A——TH, ESQ.

["Methinks I see him already in the cart, sweeter and more lovely than the nosegay in his hand! I hear the crowd extolling his resolution and intrepidity! What volleys of sighs are sent from the windows of Holborn, that so comely a youth should be brought to disgrace! I see him at the tree! the whole circle are in tears! even butchers weep!"
— BEGGARS' OPERA.]

A LIVING sea of eager human faces,
   A thousand bosoms throbbing all as one,
Walls, windows, balconies, all sorts of places,
   Holding their crowds of gazers to the sun :
     Through the hushed groups low-buzzing murmurs run ;
And on the air, with slow reluctant swell,
Comes the dull funeral-boom of old Sepulchre's bell.

Oh, joy in London now ! in festal measure
   Be spent the evening of this festive day !

For thee is opening now a high-strung pleasure;
   Now, even now, in yonder press-yard they
   Strike from his limbs the fetters loose away!
A little while, and he, the brave Duval,
Will issue forth, serene, to glad and greet you all.

"Why comes he not? Say, wherefore doth he tarry?"
   Starts the inquiry loud from every tongue.
"Surely," they cry, "that tedious Ordinary
   His tedious psalms must long ere this have sung,—
   Tedious to him that's waiting to be hung!"
But hark! old Newgate's doors fly wide apart.
"He comes, he comes!" A thrill shoots through each gazer's heart.

Joined in the stunning cry ten thousand voices,
   All Smithfield answered to the loud acclaim.
"He comes, he comes!" and every breast rejoices,
   As down Snow Hill the shout tumultuous came,
   Bearing to Holborn's crowd the welcome fame.
"He comes, he comes!" and each holds back his breath—
Some ribs are broke, and some few scores are crushed to death.

With step majestic to the cart advances
  The dauntless Claude, and springs into his seat.
He feels that on him now are fixed the glances
  Of many a Briton bold and maiden sweet,
  Whose hearts responsive to his glories beat.
In him the honour of "The Road" is centred,
And all the hero's fire into his bosom entered.

His was the transport—his the exultation
  Of Rome's great generals, when from afar,
Up to the Capitol, in the ovation,
  They bore with them, in the triumphal car,
  Rich gold and gems, the spoils of foreign war.
Io Triumphe! They forgot their clay.
E'en so Duval, who rode in glory on his way.

His laced cravat, his kids of purest yellow,
  The many-tinted nosegay in his hand,
His large black eyes, so fiery, yet so mellow,
  Like the old vintages of Spanish land,
  Locks clustering o'er a brow of high command,
Subdue all hearts; and, as up Holborn's steep
Toils the slow car of death, e'en cruel butchers weep.

He saw it, but he heeded not. His story,
　　He knew, was graven on the page of Time.
Tyburn to him was as a field of glory,
　　Where he must stoop to death his head sublime,
　　Hymned in full many an elegiac rhyme.
He left his deeds behind him, and his name—
For he, like Cæsar, had lived long enough for fame.

He quailed not, save when, as he raised the chalice,—
　　St Giles's bowl,—filled with the mildest ale,
To pledge the crowd, on her—his beauteous Alice—
　　His eye alighted, and his cheek grew pale.
　　She, whose sweet breath was like the spicy gale,
She, whom he fondly deemed his own dear girl,
Stood with a tall dragoon, drinking long draughts of
　　purl.

He bit his lip—it quivered but a moment—
　　Then passed his hand across his flushing brows:
He could have spared so forcible a comment
　　Upon the constancy of woman's vows.
　　One short sharp pang his hero-soul allows;
But in the bowl he drowned the stinging pain,
And on his pilgrim course went calmly forth again.

THE DEATH OF DUVAL.

A princely group of England's noble daughters
    Stood in a balcony suffused with grief,
Diffusing fragrance round them, of strong waters,
    And waving many a snowy handkerchief;
    Then glowed the prince of highwayman and thief!
His soul was touched with a seraphic gleam—
That woman could be false was but a mocking dream.

And now, his bright career of triumph ended,
    His chariot stood beneath the triple tree.
The law's grim finisher to its boughs ascended,
    And fixed the hempen bandages, while he
    Bowed to the throng, then bade the cart go free.
The car rolled on, and left him dangling there,
Like famed Mohammed's tomb, uphung midway in air.

As droops the cup of the surchargèd lily
    Beneath the buffets of the surly storm,
Or the soft petals of the daffodilly,
    When Sirius is uncomfortably warm,
    So drooped his head upon his manly form,
While floated in the breeze his tresses brown.
He hung the stated time, and then they cut him down.

With soft and tender care the trainbands bore him,
    Just as they found him, nightcap, robe, and all,
And placed this neat though plain inscription o'er him,
    Among the atomies in Surgeons' Hall:
    "THESE ARE THE BONES OF THE RENOWNED DUVAL!"
There still they tell us, from their glassy case,
He was the last, the best of all that noble race!

Eastern Serenade.

The minarets wave on the plain of Stamboul,
And the breeze of the evening blows freshly and cool;
The voice of the musnud is heard from the west,
And kaftan and kalpac have gone to their rest.
The notes of the kislar re-echo no more,
And the waves of Al Sirat fall light on the shore.

Where art thou, my beauty; where art thou, my bride?
Oh, come and repose by thy dragoman's side!
I wait for thee still by the flowery tophaik—
I have broken my Eblis for Zuleima's sake.
But the heart that adores thee is faithful and true,
Though it beats 'neath the folds of a Greek Allah-hu!

Oh, wake thee, my dearest! the muftis are still,
And the tschocadars sleep on the Franguestan hill;
No sullen alcikoum—no derveesh is here,
And the mosques are all watching by lonely Kashmere!
Oh, come in the gush of thy beauty so full,
I have waited for thee, my adored attar-gul!

I see thee—I hear thee—thy antelope foot
Treads lightly and soft on the velvet cheroot;
The jewelled amaun of thy zemzem is bare,
And the folds of thy palampore wave in the air.
Come, rest on the bosom that loves thee so well,
My dove! my phingari! my gentle gazelle!

Nay, tremble not, dearest! I feel thy heart throb,
'Neath the sheltering shroud of thy snowy kicbaub;

EASTERN SERENADE.

Lo, there shines Muezzin, the beautiful star!
Thy lover is with thee, and danger afar:
Say, is it the glance of the haughty vizier,
Or the bark of the distant effendi, you fear?

Oh, swift fly the hours in the garden of bliss!
And sweeter than balm of Gehenna thy kiss!
Wherever I wander—wherever I roam,
My spirit flies back to its beautiful home;
It dwells by the lake of the limpid Stamboul,
With thee, my adored one! my own attar-gul!

Dame Fredegonde.

When folks, with headstrong passion blind,
To play the fool make up their mind,
They're sure to come with phrases nice
And modest air, for your advice.
But as a truth unfailing make it,
They ask, but never mean to take it.
'Tis not advice they want, in fact,
But confirmation in their act.
Now mark what did, in such a case,
A worthy priest who knew the race.

A dame more buxom, blithe, and free,
Than Fredegonde you scarce would see.
So smart her dress, so trim her shape,
Ne'er hostess offered juice of grape,
Could for her trade wish better sign;
Her looks gave flavour to her wine,

And each guest feels it, as he sips,
Smack of the ruby of her lips.
A smile for all, a welcome glad,—
A jovial coaxing way she had;
And,—what was more her fate than blame,—
A nine months' widow was our dame.
But toil was hard, for trade was good,
And gallants sometimes will be rude.
"And what can a lone woman do?
The nights are long and eerie too.
Now, Guillot there's a likely man,
None better draws or taps a can;
He's just the man, I think, to suit,
If I could bring my courage to't."
With thoughts like these her mind is crossed:
The dame, they say, who doubts, is lost.
"But then the risk? I'll beg a slice
Of Father Raulin's good advice."

Prankt in her best, with looks demure,
She seeks the priest; and, to be sure,
Asks if he thinks she ought to wed:

"With such a business on my head,
I'm worried off my legs with care,
And need some help to keep things square.
I've thought of Guillot, truth to tell!
He's steady, knows his business well.
What do you think?" When thus he met her:
"Oh, take him, dear, you can't do better!"
"But then the danger, my good pastor,
If of the man I make the master.
There is no trusting to these men."
"Well, well, my dear, don't have him, then!"
"But help I must have; there's the curse.
I may go farther and fare worse."
"Why, take him, then!" "But if he should
Turn out a thankless ne'er-do-good—
In drink and riot waste my all,
And rout me out of house and hall?"
"Don't have him, then! But I've a plan
To clear your doubts, if any can.
The bells a peal are ringing,—hark!
Go straight, and what they tell you mark.
If they say 'Yes!' wed, and be blest—
If 'No,' why—do as you think best."

The bells rang out a triple bob:
Oh, how our widow's heart did throb,
As thus she heard their burden go,
"Marry, mar-marry, mar-Guillot!"
Bells were not then left to hang idle:
A week,—and they rang for her bridal.
But, woe the while, they might as well
Have rung the poor dame's parting knell.
The rosy dimples left her cheek,
She lost her beauties plump and sleek;
For Guillot oftener kicked than kissed,
And backed his orders with his fist,
Proving by deeds as well as words
That servants make the worst of lords.

She seeks the priest, her ire to wreak.
And speaks as angry women speak,
With tiger looks and bosom swelling,
Cursing the hour she took his telling.
To all, his calm reply was this,—
" I fear you've read the bells amiss :
If they have lead you wrong in aught,
Your wish, not they, inspired the thought.

Just go, and mark well what they say."
Off trudged the dame upon her way,
And sure enough their chime went so,—
" Don't have that knave, that knave Guillot!"

" Too true," she cried, " there's not a doubt:
What could my ears have been about?"
She had forgot, that, as fools think,
The bell is ever sure to clink.

The Death of Ishmael.

[This and the six following poems are examples of that new achievement of modern song—which, blending the *utile* with the *dulce*, symbolises at once the practical and spiritual characteristics of the age,—and is called familiarly "the puff poetical."]

DIED the Jew? "The Hebrew died.
    On the pavement cold he lay,
Around him closed the living tide;
    The butcher's cad set down his tray;
The pot-boy from the Dragon Green
    No longer for his pewter calls;
The Nereid rushes in between,
    Nor more her 'Fine live mackerel!' bawls."

Died the Jew? "The Hebrew died.
    They raised him gently from the stone,
They flung his coat and neckcloth wide—
    But linen had that Hebrew none.
They raised the pile of hats that pressed
    His noble head, his locks of snow;
But, ah, that head, upon his breast,
    Sank down with an expiring 'Clo!'"

Died the Jew? "The Hebrew died,
    Struck with overwhelming qualms
From the flavour spreading wide
    Of some fine Virginia hams.
Would you know the fatal spot,
    Fatal to that child of sin?
These fine-flavoured hams are bought
    At 50 Bishopsgate Within!"

Parr's Life Pills.

'Twas in the town of Lubeck,
    A hundred years ago,
An old man walked into the church,
    With beard as white as snow;
Yet were his cheeks not wrinkled,
    Nor dim his eagle eye:
There's many a knight that steps the street,
Might wonder, should he chance to meet
    That man erect and high!

When silenced was the organ,
    And hushed the vespers loud,
The Sacristan approached the sire,
    And drew him from the crowd—
"There's something in thy visage,

On which I dare not look;
And when I rang the passing bell,
A tremor that I may not tell,
My very vitals shook.

"Who art thou, awful stranger?
Our ancient annals say,
That twice two hundred years ago
Another passed this way,
Like thee in face and feature;
And, if the tale be true,
'Tis writ, that in this very year
Again the stranger shall appear.
Art thou the Wandering Jew?"

"The Wandering Jew, thou dotard!"
The wondrous phantom cried—
"'Tis several centuries ago
Since that poor stripling died.
He would not use my nostrums—

See, shaveling, here they are!
These put to flight all human ills,
These conquer death—unfailing pills,
And I'm the inventor, PARR!"

Tarquin and the Augur.

GINGERLY is good King Tarquin shaving.
    Gently glides the razor o'er his chin,
Near him stands a grim Haruspex raving,
    And with nasal whine he pitches in
        Church extension hints,
        Till the monarch squints,
Snicks his chin, and swears—a deadly sin!

"Jove confound thee, thou bare-legged impostor!
    From my dressing-table get thee gone!
Dost thou think my flesh is double Glo'ster?
    There again! That cut was to the bone!
        Get ye from my sight;
        I'll believe you're right,
When my razor cuts the sharpening hone!"

TARQUIN AND THE AUGUR.

Thus spoke Tarquin with a deal of dryness;
    But the Augur, eager for his fees,
Answered—"Try it, your Imperial Highness;
    Press a little harder, if you please.
        There! the deed is done!"
        Through the solid stone
Went the steel as glibly as through cheese.

So the Augur touched the tin of Tarquin,
    Who suspected some celestial aid;
But he wronged the blameless gods; for hearken!
    Ere the monarch's bet was rashly laid,
        With his searching eye
        Did the priest espy
ROGERS' name engraved upon the blade.

La Mort d'Arthur.

NOT BY ALFRED TENNYSON.

SLOWLY, as one who bears a mortal hurt,
Through which the fountain of his life runs dry,
Crept good King Arthur down unto the lake.
A roughening wind was bringing in the waves
With cold dull plash and plunging to the shore,
And a great bank of clouds came sailing up
Athwart the aspect of the gibbous moon,
Leaving no glimpse save starlight, as he sank,
With a short stagger, senseless on the stones.

No man yet knows how long he lay in swound;
But long enough it was to let the rust
Lick half the surface of his polished shield;
For it was made by far inferior hands,
Than forged his helm, his breastplate, and his greaves,
Whereon no canker lighted, for they bore
The magic stamp of MECHI'S SILVER STEEL.

Jupiter and the Indian Ale.

"Take away this clammy nectar!"
　Said the king of gods and men;
"Never at Olympus' table
　Let that trash be served again.

Ho, Lyæus, thou the beery!
    Quick—invent some other drink;
Or, in a brace of shakes, thou standest
    On Cocytus' sulphury brink!"

Terror shook the limbs of Bacchus,
    Paly grew his pimpled nose,
And already in his rearward
    Felt he Jove's tremendous toes;
When a bright idea struck him—
    "Dash my thyrsus! I'll be bail—
For you never were in India—
    That you know not Hodgson's Ale!"

"Bring it!" quoth the Cloud-compeller;
    And the wine-god brought the beer—
"Port and claret are like water
    To the noble stuff that's here!"

And Saturnius drank and nodded,
    Winking with his lightning eyes,
And amidst the constellations
    Did the star of Hodgson rise!

The Lay of the Doudney Brothers.

COATS at five-and-forty shillings! trousers ten-and-six a pair!

Summer waistcoats, three a sov'reign, light and comfortable wear!

Taglionis, black or coloured, Chesterfield and velveteen!

The old English shooting-jacket—doeskins such as ne'er were seen!

Army cloaks and riding-habits, Alberts at a trifling cost!

Do you want an annual contract? Write to DOUDNEYS' by the post.

DOUDNEY BROTHERS! DOUDNEY BROTHERS! Not the men that drive the van,

Plastered o'er with advertisements, heralding some paltry plan,

How, by base mechanic stinting, and by pinching of
    their backs,
Lean attorneys' clerks may manage to retrieve their
    Income-tax:
But the old established business—where the best of
    clothes are given
At the very lowest prices—Fleet Street, Number
    Ninety-seven.
Wouldst thou know the works of DOUDNEY? Hie
    thee to the thronged Arcade,
To the Park upon a Sunday, to the terrible Parade.
There, amid the bayonets bristling, and the flashing
    of the steel,
When the household troops in squadrons round the
    bold field-marshals wheel,
Shouldst thou see an aged warrior in a plain blue
    morning frock,
Peering at the proud battalions o'er the margin of his
    stock,—
Should thy throbbing heart then tell thee, that the
    veteran worn and grey
Curbed the course of Bonaparte, rolled the thunders
    of Assaye—

Let it tell thee, stranger, likewise, that the goodly
 garb he wears
Started into shape and being from the DOUDNEY
 BROTHERS' shears!
Seek thou next the rooms of Willis—mark, where
 D'Orsay's Count is bending,
See the trouser's undulation from his graceful hip
 descending;
Hath the earth another trouser so compact and love-
 compelling?
Thou canst find it, stranger, only, if thou seek'st the
 DOUDNEYS' dwelling!
Hark, from Windsor's royal palace, what sweet voice
 enchants the ear?
"Goodness, what a lovely waistcoat! Oh, who made
 it, Albert dear?
'Tis the very prettiest pattern! You must get a
 dozen others!"
And the Prince, in rapture, answers—"'Tis the work
 of DOUDNEY BROTHERS!"

Paris and Helen.

As the youthful Paris presses
    Helen to his ivory breast,
Sporting with her golden tresses,
    Close and ever closer pressed,

" Let me," said he, " quaff the nectar,
    Which thy lips of ruby yield;
Glory I can leave to Hector,
    Gathered in the tented field.

" Let me ever gaze upon thee,
    Look into thine eyes so deep;
With a daring hand I won thee,
    With a faithful heart I'll keep.

" Oh, my Helen, thou bright wonder,
    Who was ever like to thee?
Jove would lay aside his thunder,
    So he might be blest like me.

"How mine eyes so fondly linger
   On thy soft and pearly skin;
Scan each round and rosy finger,
   Drinking draughts of beauty in!

"Tell me, whence thy beauty, fairest?
   Whence thy cheek's enchanting bloom?
Whence the rosy hue thou wearest;
   Breathing round thee rich perfume?"

Thus he spoke, with heart that panted,
   Clasped her fondly to his side,
Gazed on her with look enchanted,
   While his Helen thus replied:

"Be no discord, love, between us,
   If I not the secret tell!
'Twas a gift I had of Venus,—
   Venus, who hath loved me well;

"And she told me as she gave it,
   'Let not e'er the charm be known;
O'er thy person freely lave it,
   Only when thou art alone.'

"'Tis enclosed in yonder casket—
    Here behold its golden key;
But its name—love, do not ask it,
    Tell't I may not, even to thee!"

Long with vow and kiss he plied her;
    Still the secret did she keep,
Till at length he sank beside her,
    Seemed as he had dropped to sleep.

Soon was Helen laid in slumber,
    When her Paris, rising slow,
Did his fair neck disencumber
    From her rounded arms of snow.

Then, her heedless fingers oping,
    Takes the key and steals away,
To the ebon table groping,
    Where the wondrous casket lay;

Eagerly the lid uncloses,
    Sees within it, laid aslope,
PEARS' LIQUID BLOOM OF ROSES,
    Cakes of his TRANSPARENT SOAP!

Song of the Ennuyé.

I'm weary, and sick, and disgusted
    With Britain's mechanical din;
Where I'm much too well known to be trusted,
    And plaguily pestered for tin;
Where love has two eyes for your banker,
    And one chilly glance for yourself;
Where souls can afford to be franker,
    But when they're well garnished with pelf.

I'm sick of the whole race of poets,
    Emasculate, misty, and fine;
They brew their small-beer, and don't know its
    Distinction from full-bodied wine.
I'm sick of the prosers, that house up
    At drowsy St Stephen's,—ain't you?
I want some strong spirits to rouse up
    A good revolution or two!

SONG OF THE ENNUYÉ.

I'm sick of a land, where each morrow
    Repeats the dull tale of to-day,
Where you can't even find a new sorrow
    To chase your stale pleasures away.
I'm sick of blue-stockings horrific,
    Steam, railroads, gas, scrip, and consols;
So I'll off where the golden Pacific
    Round Islands of Paradise rolls.

There the passions shall revel unfettered,
    And the heart never speak but in truth,
And the intellect, wholly unlettered,
    Be bright with the freedom of youth!
There the earth can rejoice in her blossoms,
    Unsullied by vapour or soot,
And there chimpanzees and opossums
    Shall playfully pelt me with fruit.

There I'll sit with my dark Orianas,
    In groves by the murmuring sea,
And they'll give, as I suck the bananas,
    Their kisses, nor ask them from me.

They'll never torment me for sonnets,
    Nor bore me to death with their own;
They'll ask not for shawls nor for bonnets,
    For milliners there are unknown.

There my couch shall be earth's freshest flowers,
    My curtains the night and the stars,
And my spirit shall gather new powers,
    Uncramped by conventional bars.
Love for love, truth for truth ever giving,
    My days shall be manfully sped;
I shall know that I'm loved while I'm living,
    And be wept by fond eyes when I'm dead!

Caroline.

Lightsome, brightsome, cousin mine,
    Easy, breezy Caroline!
With thy locks all raven-shaded,
From thy merry brow up-braided,
And thine eyes of laughter full,
    Brightsome cousin mine!
Thou in chains of love hast bound me—
Wherefore dost thou flit around me,
    Laughter-loving Caroline?

When I fain would go to sleep
    In my easy-chair,
Wherefore on my slumbers creep -
Wherefore start me from repose,
Tickling of my hookèd nose,
    Pulling of my hair?

Wherefore, then, if thou dost love me,
So to words of anger move me,
   Corking of this face of mine,
   Tricksy cousin Caroline?

When a sudden sound I hear,
Much my nervous system suffers,
   Shaking through and through.
Cousin Caroline, I fear,
   'Twas no other, now, but you,
Put gunpowder in the snuffers,
   Springing such a mine!
Yes, it was your tricksy self,
Wicked-trickèd little elf,
   Naughty Caroline!

Pins she sticks into my shoulder,
   Places needles in my chair,
And, when I begin to scold her,
   Tosses back her combèd hair,
   With so saucy-vexed an air,
That the pitying beholder
Cannot brook that I should scold her:

Then again she comes, and bolder,
    Blacks anew this face of mine,
    Artful cousin Caroline!

Would she only say she'd love me,
    Winsome, tinsome Caroline,
Unto such excess 'twould move me,
    Teazing, pleasing, cousin mine!
That she might the live-long day
Undermine the snuffer-tray,
Tickle still my hookèd nose,
Startle me from calm repose
    With her pretty persecution;
Throw the tongs against my shins,
Run me through and through with pins,
    Like a piercèd cushion;
Would she only say she'd love me,
Darning-needles should not move me;
But, reclining back, I'd say,
"Dearest! there's the snuffer-tray;
Pinch, O pinch those legs of mine!
Cork me, cousin Caroline!"

To a Forget-Me-Not,

FOUND IN MY EMPORIUM OF LOVE-TOKENS.

Sweet flower, that with thy soft blue eye
    Didst once look up in shady spot,
To whisper to the passer-by
    Those tender words—Forget-me-not!

Though withered now, thou art to me
    The minister of gentle thought,—
And I could weep to gaze on thee,
    Love's faded pledge—Forget-me-not!

Thou speak'st of hours when I was young,
    And happiness arose unsought;
When she, the whispering woods among,
    Gave me thy bloom—Forget-me-not!

That rapturous hour with that dear maid
    From memory's page no time shall blot,
When, yielding to my kiss, she said,
    " Oh, Theodore—Forget me not!"

Alas for love! alas for truth!
    Alas for man's uncertain lot!
Alas for all the hopes of youth
    That fade like thee—Forget-me-not!

Alas for that one image fair,
    With all my brightest dreams inwrought!
That walks beside me everywhere,
    Still whispering—Forget-me-not!

Oh, Memory! thou art but a sigh
    For friendships dead and loves forgot,
And many a cold and altered eye
    That once did say—Forget-me-not!

And I must bow me to thy laws,
    For—odd although it may be thought—
I can't tell who the deuce it was
    That gave me this Forget-me-not!

The Mishap.

"Why art thou weeping, sister?
    Why is thy cheek so pale?
Look up, dear Jane, and tell me
    What is it thou dost ail?

"I know thy will is froward,
    Thy feelings warm and keen,
And that *that* Augustus Howard
    For weeks has not been seen.

"I know how much you loved him;
　　But I know thou dost not weep
For him;—for though his passion be,
　　His purse is noways deep.

"Then tell me why those tear-drops?
　　What means this woeful mood?
Say, has the tax-collector
　　Been calling, and been rude?

"Or has that hateful grocer,
　　The slave! been here to-day?
Of course he had, by morrow's noon,
　　A heavy bill to pay!

"Come, on thy brother's bosom
　　Unburden all thy woes;
Look up, look up, sweet sister;
　　Nay, sob not through thy nose."

"Oh, John, 'tis not the grocer
　　Or his account, although
How ever he is to be paid
　　I really do not know.

" 'Tis not the tax-collector;
　　Though by his fell command
They've seized our old paternal clock,
　　And new umbrella-stand!

" Nor that Augustus Howard,
　　Whom I despise almost,—
But the soot's come down the chimney, John,
　　And fairly spoilt the roast!"

Comfort in Affliction.

" Wherefore starts my bosom's lord?
    Why this anguish in thine eye?
Oh, it seems as thy heart's chord
    Had broken with that sigh!

" Rest thee, my dear lord, I pray,
    Rest thee on my bosom now!
And let me wipe the dews away,
    Are gathering on thy brow.

" There, again! that fevered start!
    What, love! husband! is thy pain?
There is a sorrow on thy heart,
    A weight upon thy brain!

" Nay, nay, that sickly smile can ne'er
    Deceive affection's searching eye;
'Tis a wife's duty, love, to share
    Her husband's agony.

"Since the dawn began to peep,
    Have I lain with stifled breath;
Heard thee moaning in thy sleep,
    As thou wert at grips with death.

"Oh, what joy it was to see
    My gentle lord once more awake!
Tell me, what is amiss with thee?
    Speak, or my heart will break!"

"Mary, thou angel of my life,
    Thou ever good and kind;
'Tis not, believe me, my dear wife,
    The anguish of the mind!

"It is not in my bosom, dear,
    No, nor my brain, in sooth;
But Mary, oh, I feel it here,
    Here in my wisdom tooth!

"Then give,—oh, first best antidote,—
    Sweet partner of my bed!
Give me thy flannel petticoat
    To wrap around my head!"

The Invocation.

" Brother, thou art very weary,
    And thine eye is sunk and dim,
And thy neckcloth's tie is crumpled,
    And thy collar out of trim;
There is dust upon thy visage,—
    Think not, Charles, I would hurt ye,
When I say, that altogether
    You appear extremely dirty.

" Frown not, brother, now, but hie thee
    To thy chamber's distant room;
Drown the odours of the ledger
    With the lavender's perfume.
Brush the mud from off thy trousers,
    O'er the china basin kneel,
Lave thy brows in water softened
    With the soap of Old Castile.

"Smooth the locks that o'er thy forehead
    Now in loose disorder stray;
Pare thy nails, and from thy whiskers
    Cut those ragged points away;
Let no more thy calculations
    Thy bewildered brain beset;
Life has other hopes than Cocker's,
    Other joys than tare and tret.

"Haste thee, for I ordered dinner,
    Waiting to the very last,
Twenty minutes after seven,
    And 'tis now the quarter past.
'Tis a dinner which Lucullus
    Would have wept with joy to see,
One, might wake the soul of Curtis
    From death's drowsy atrophy.

"There is soup of real turtle,
    Turbot, and the dainty sole;
And the mottled roe of lobsters
    Blushes through the butter-bowl.

There the lordly haunch of mutton,
    Tender as the mountain grass,
Waits to mix its ruddy juices
    With the girdling caper-sauce.

"There a stag, whose branching forehead
    Spoke him monarch of the herds,
He whose flight was o'er the heather
    Swift as through the air the bird's,
Yields for thee a dish of cutlets;
    And the haunch that wont to dash
O'er the roaring mountain-torrent,
    Smokes in most delicious hash.

"There, besides, are amber jellies
    Floating like a golden dream;
Ginger from the far Bermudas,
    Dishes of Italian cream;
And a princely apple-dumpling,
    Which my own fair fingers wrought,
Shall unfold its nectared treasures
    To thy lips all smoking hot.

"Ha! I see thy brow is clearing,
    Lustre flashes from thine eyes;
To thy lips I see the moisture
    Of anticipation rise.
Hark! the dinner-bell is sounding!
    "Only wait one moment, Jane:
I'll be dressed, and down, before you
    Can get up the iced champagne!"

The Husband's Petition.

Come hither, my heart's darling,
    Come, sit upon my knee,
And listen, while I whisper
    A boon I ask of thee.
You need not pull my whiskers
    So amorously, my dove;
'Tis something quite apart from
    The gentle cares of love.

I feel a bitter craving—
　　A dark and deep desire,
That glows beneath my bosom
　　Like coals of kindled fire.
The passion of the nightingale,
　　When singing to the rose,
Is feebler than the agony
　　That murders my repose!

Nay, dearest! do not doubt me,
　　Though madly thus I speak—
I feel thy arms about me,
　　Thy tresses on my cheek:
I know the sweet devotion
　　That links thy heart with mine,—
I know my soul's emotion
　　Is doubly felt by thine:

And deem not that a shadow
　　Hath fallen across my love:
No, sweet, my love is shadowless,
　　As yonder heaven above.

These little taper fingers—
　Ah, Jane! how white they be!—
Can well supply the cruel want
　That almost maddens me.

Thou wilt not sure deny me
　My first and fond request;
I pray thee, by the memory
　Of all we cherish best—
By all the dear remembrance
　Of those delicious days,
When, hand in hand, we wandered
　Along the summer braes;

By all we felt, unspoken,
　When 'neath the early moon,
We sat beside the rivulet,
　In the leafy month of June;
And by the broken whisper
　That fell upon my ear,
More sweet than angel music,
　When first I wooed thee, dear!

By thy great vow which bound thee
    For ever to my side,
And by the ring that made thee
    My darling and my bride!
Thou wilt not fail nor falter,
    But bend thee to the task—
A BOILED SHEEP'S-HEAD ON SUNDAY
    Is all the boon I ask!

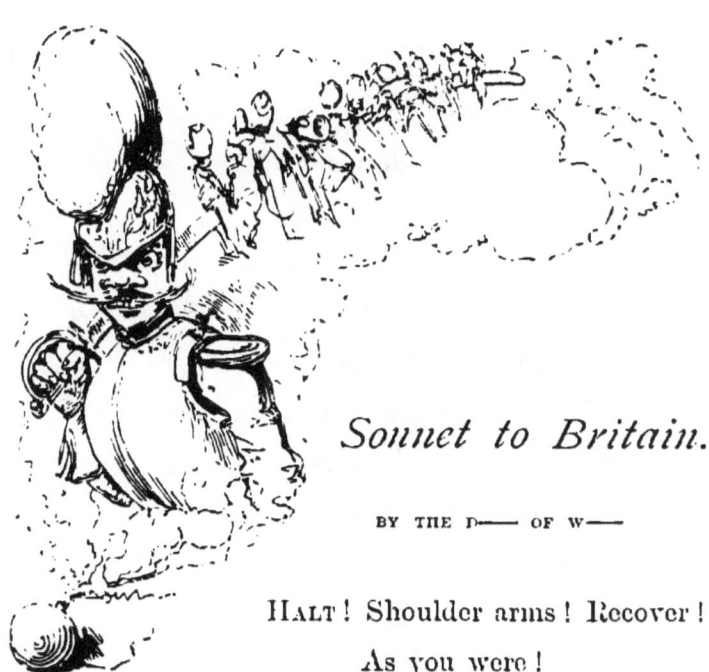

Sonnet to Britain.

BY THE D—— OF W——

HALT! Shoulder arms! Recover!
　　As you were!
　Right wheel!　Eyes left!　Attention!
　　Stand at ease!
O Britain!　O my country!　Words like these
　Have made thy name a terror and a fear
To all the nations.　Witness Ebro's banks,

Assaye, Toulouse, Nivelle, and Waterloo,
   Where the grim despot muttered—*Sauve qui peut!*
And Ney fled darkling.—Silence in the ranks!
Inspired by these, amidst the iron crash
   Of armies, in the centre of his troop
The soldier stands—unmovable, not rash—
   Until the forces of the foeman droop;
Then knocks the Frenchmen to eternal smash,
   Pounding them into mummy. Shoulder, hoop!

THE END.

PRINTED BY WILLIAM BLACKWOOD AND SONS.

www.ingramcontent.com/pod-product-compliance
Lightning Source LLC
Chambersburg PA
CBHW032044230426
43672CB00009B/1459